JOSEPH WILLIAMS

SHEEP IN

WOLVES'

CLOTHING

The Negro National Anthem

Lift each voice and sing
Till earth and heaven ring,
Ring with the harmonies of Liberty;
Let our rejoicing rise
High as the listening skies,
Let it resound loud as the rolling sea.
Sing a song full of the faith that the dark past has taught us,
Sing a song full of the hope that the present has brought us,
Facing the rising sun of our new day begun
Let us march on till victory is won.

So begins the Black National Anthem, by James Weldon Johnson in 1900. Lift Every Voice is the name of the joint imprint of the Institute for Black Family Development and Moody Press, a division of the Moody Bible Institute.

Our vision is to advance the cause of Christ through publishing African American Christians who educate, edify and disciple Christians in the church community through quality books written for African Americans.

The Institute for Black Family Development is a national Christian organization. It offers degreed and non-degreed training nationally and internationally to established and emerging leaders from churches and Christian organizations. To learn more about the Institute for Black Family Development write us at:

The Institute for Black Family Development
15151 Faust
Detroit, Michigan 48223

Moody Press, a ministry of Moody Bible Institute,
is designed for education, evangelization, and edification.
If we may assist you in knowing more about Christ
and the Christian life, please write us without obligation:

Moody Press
c/o Moody Literature Ministries
820 N. LaSalle Blvd.
Chicago, Illinois 60610

JOSEPH WILLIAMS

SHEEP IN

WHEN THE ACTIONS

WOLVES'

OF A CHRISTIAN

CLOTHING

TURN CRIMINAL

All Scripture quotations are taken from the King James Version.

ISBN: 0-8024-6594-3

1 3 5 7 9 10 8 6 4 2
Printed in the United States of America

In memory of my parents, Robert Williams, Sr. and Annie Bell Slappy-Williams and my adoptive parents, Flim and Freddie Brooks.

To my wife Sharon, my lover, my best friend, my soul's mate—Thank you for loving me and believing in me.

To my son Anthony (Tony)—you are my inspiration.

To my son Stephen—you are my hope.

To my daughter AnnDrea—you are my joy.

To my daughter Gabrielle—you are my delight

Contents

Acknowledgments

There are son many people to thank for helping me make it to this point and in making the writing of this humble book become a reality. First of all, thanks to my extended family and the church family at Greater New Mt. Moriah Missionary Baptist Church, especially the Saturday prayer group, the Sunday School department and my spiritual mother, Henrietta Barney, for helping me in my transition from a life of crime and drugs to a life of faith. Thanks to Rev. Robert Joe Paige for encouraging me in the ministry. Thanks to Oddis Lewis for instilling in me a love and excitement for God's Word. Thanks to Rev. Frank Raines, Jr. for challenging me to study God's Word in depth. Thanks to Matthew Parker, my teacher, mentor and friend for helping to get this book publised. Thanks to Fred Zillich of CBMC for teaching me how to give a personal testimony that glorifies God and for opening the door for me to become a national speaker with CBMC. Thanks to my sister, Amanda Johnson for encouraging me to finish the manuscript. Thanks to Eugene Seals for your encouragment and help. Thanks to my co-worker, Marilynn Tenore for proofing the first draft of the manuscript. Thanks to all the others who have encouraged, mentored and helped me in so many ways over the years.

Foreword

I n the work of Prison Fellowship, we participate in special ways in proclaiming the good news of transformation through Jesus Christ. Joe Williams' story is a profound witness to that news. If I did not hear it from his own testimony, I would have never believed that the colleague I know had lived the life described in this book. Yet God has used even the degradation of drug addiction to show His power in Joe's life and to others through him. I have known Joe since the early 1990s as a strong leader nearly tireless in serving Jesus Christ. It has been my privilege to serve with him in Prison Fellowship. I will never forget the day Joe accompanied me to Lansing for a visit with Governor John Engler and his top staff to talk about ways the state can do a better job with corrections. Joe looked every bit the executive, right down to the cufflinks. He spoke knowledgeably about his work with ex-prisoners in transition and what programs really make a difference. It was in a discussion about the value of prison programs that teach inmates a trade that the thunderbolt came. The consensus around that shining mahogany table was that it does no good to provide job training in prison. Then Joe quietly spoke up to say that if he had not learned the upholstery trade in prison at Fort Leavenworth, he would not be there that day. I looked around the table and realized how difficult it was for the top leaders of the state of Michigan to believe that the man before them had been a prisoner whom no one would have given the least odds of making it into a governor's office. And yet, there he was. It changed the entire discussion, and Joe's comments commanded a new level of respect and credibility.

In his introduction to this book, Joe expresses the desire that readers in despair about their own lives or those of loved ones caught up in wolfish lifestyles will find hope. Indeed there is hope, because the Good Shepherd is at work to seek and to save—in His own way and time—His sheep that are lost and to redeem their wasted days for His own great purpose.

Thomas C. Pratt, President
Prison Fellowship Ministries

Introduction

B am bam bam!!! came the loud raps on the gray, metal-covered, military door. "Killer, get up and answer the door," Crack shouted through the door in his gravely Midwestern ghetto dialect. As I struggled to shake myself out of the deep stupor, I realized that my clothing and mattress were saturated with urine and perspiration. Actually, fluid leaked from every pore and opening of my body. Mucous had drained from my nasal passage and now had settled in my throat, making it necessary for me to cough several times before I could utter an intelligible sound. My limbs shook uncontrollably as I tried to gain control of my pain-wracked body.

"Yeah, yeah, I'm comin', I'm comin'," I replied in shaky tones. The depth of the heroin withdrawal symptoms made it difficult for my legs to support my weight as I shuffled to the door. I quickly retreated to my bed as Crack and Brad entered the semi-private room in an old converted Nazi barracks housing the field artillery battery to which I was assigned. I sank down onto the bed, preventing anyone else sitting on it and discovering I had lost control of my bladder. The dimly lit room concealed the urine and perspiration stains on my olive drab-colored fatigues, or so I thought. Nothing, however, could hide the stench of the urine and perspiration-soaked fabric. At that moment, I felt like I had been run over by a Mack truck and then dragged through a slime pit. My two visitors seemed oblivious to my shameful condition.

"What's happenin' y'all? I'm sick as a dog. I need a "do" (fix) badder (worse) than a dead man needs a coffin. Y'all got up on any duji (heroin) yet?"

"Git yo' clothes on, man," replied Crack. "Brad ran across some white boys over in the next barracks who say they got some mean stuff."

I leaped to my feet and hurried to my locker, retrieving a pair of clean fatigues. Peeling off the filthy uniform and stuffing it into my laundry bag, I donned my clean fatigues without removing my damp cotton underwear. "Let's go," I muttered, moving toward the door. We filed out of the room together and into the brightly lit hallway. My eyes automatically squinted to block out the bright fluorescent light. Down the stairs and out the front door we traveled, our faces grim and deadly serious. Brad directed us to the room where the would-be GI drug dealers had set up shop. None of us had enough money to satisfy the cravings of even one deeply addicted heroin user. We knew our drill so well we didn't even need to rehearse our actions.

After being allowed to enter the room by the occupants, I made a quick but casual sweep of the room, noting three individuals present. This would be easy work, I thought. Brad explained to the man who appeared to be in charge that we were interested in purchasing a sizable quantity of his product. Naturally, we would all need a sample before we could make a decision to buy their product.

Because my condition was the worst of all my companions, it was agreed that I would be the first to "get off" (shoot up). I set my "works" (syringe, needle, and cooker) on top of the footlocker that served as a makeshift coffee table. My cooker consisted of a large spoon I had pilfered from the mess hall. Our host dumped a generous portion of his product into the cooker. With my syringe I intuitively drew up just the correct amount of water from the cup that had been provided for us. Most of the white powder dissolved after the water had been applied to it. This meant the heroin was nearly pure in quality. The flame of a Bic lighter was used to dissolve the rest of the powder into the liquid. The aroma of the sizzling formula was sweeter to me than the aroma of Mamma's famous peach cobbler baking in the oven on a Sunday afternoon. Crack applied a vicelike grip to the slender biceps of my left arm, causing the veins in my arm to stand at attention. With the skill of a physician, I tapped the point of the half-inch needle into a familiar spot. With the tip of my index finger, I pulled the plunger of the syringe slightly back. I watched with joy and relief as the dark red blood streamed into the cylinder of the syringe and mixed with the heroin and water mixture. Satisfied that I had a good "hit" (the needle was securely in the vein), I slowly pushed the hot liquid out of the needle and into my bloodstream.

The hot drug coursed up my arm. Within seconds the knot in my stomach quickly relaxed. A faint sigh of relief escaped my lips as the drug made its way through my body. Its effects were felt in every part of my body through which it traveled—my legs, feet, chest, and finally my brain. The healing effects of the drug were now complete. This was the moment for which I now lived. In an attempt to gain added psychological pleasure, I continued to draw the blood back and forth into the syringe, a practice heroin users refer to as "jacking off."

Crack went through the identical ritual to relieve his own withdrawal symptoms. Brad was the least strung-out of the group, so he graciously deferred his pain relief until last—dopefiend etiquette, you might say. For a brief moment, we three GI junkies enjoyed the first minutes of our altered state. This, though, was not merely an occasion for pleasure. This was also a business call.

Crack stood up slowly, signaling that it was now time to go to work. Feeling Crack's movement, Brad and I got up from our seats. Crack leaned over and slapped the man in charge hard across the face. An expression of pain and terror came over his now beet-red face. Brad and I grabbed the other two by their collars and held them at bay while Crack continued to work.

"Punk, where's the rest of the dope?" Crack demanded. The man appeared to be in shock. "If you make me ask you one more time, I'll stomp your guts out," Crack assured him, reenforcing his point by grabbing him around the neck and shaking him violently. Crack let him go so that he could go to his stash to retrieve the baggie filled with the precious white powder we sought. Having seen the force of the blow with which Crack had struck their friend, the other two young men offered no resistance. We uttered a barrage of obscenities as we backed out of the room, warning the trio what would happen if they tried to retaliate or report our actions to the authorities.

This scene would be repeated on many occasions until I was finally arrested by the German police and thrown into prison for robbery. Sitting in the solitude of a modern prison cell in Stuttgart, West Germany, for several days, I would contemplate my state and my likely fate. How had I ended up in such a state? How had a former honor student, former church youth usher, and apparently bright young Christian teenager turned into a cold-blooded predator? In only a few short years, I had unwittingly succeeded in turning from a plump-cheeked adolescent into a career criminal. Even serving a term in the military did not hamper my criminal activities. I had turned from a Christian into a criminal, from a precious lamb into a ferocious predator—a "sheep in wolves' clothing."

I'm not certain when and where the phrase "sheep in wolves' clothing" originated. The first time I heard the phrase was after I shared a part of my personal testimony with my friend and then co-worker, Bill Bracco. I had told him how I had spent thirteen years as a substance abuser, ten of those years as a hard-core heroin addict. I also shared with him that, before that experience, I had made what I feel was a genuine decision to accept Jesus Christ as Savior when I was nine years old. My drug abuse problem began when I was fifteen.

In his usual insightful manner, Bill observed that I had been what he referred to as a sheep in wolves' clothing. The phrase is obviously a turnaround of a phrase used by Jesus in Matthew 7:15 ("Beware of false prophets, which come to you in sheep's clothing, but inwardly they are ravening wolves") to refer to those who pretend to be believers so they can mingle with the flock of God in order to carry out devious schemes. The wolves are the nonbelievers. The sheep are the believers.

What an interesting analogy. To move about in Christian circles, He says that wolves would go to some lengths to disguise themselves as sheep. Can you imagine a wolf taking a bath so that he loses his wolf smell, making a sheep suit so that he resembles a sheep, even spraying on sheep cologne in order to smell like a sheep, all so he can fool the sheep into thinking that he is one of them? As bizarre as this may sound, the truth is often stranger than fiction.

On the other hand, a sheep in wolves' clothing does just the opposite. The sheep is the one who tries to rid himself of his natural (spiritual) smell. He puts on wolf clothes in order to look like a wolf. He splashes on wolf cologne in order to smell like a wolf. He learns to make wolf sounds and talk like a wolf.

As a sheep in wolves' clothing, I did all those things to pass myself off as a wolf. Somehow I had become convinced that it was more desirable to be a wolf than a sheep. Once this idea became firmly planted in my mind, I began to detest the idea of being a sheep. I began to look upon other sheep as being weird. I wanted to disassociate myself from the sheep. I wanted to lose all of my sheeply characteristics, sheeply dress, and sheeply habits. I wanted to be a wolf. Finally, I succeeded in convincing others and myself that I was a wolf.

Fortunately, I was blessed to have a godly woman as a mother. Because of her, I experienced a period of spiritual growth as a youngster. Mamma would wake me up about six o'clock in the morning after Dad had gone off to work. He worked the first shift at Ford Motor Company. After a hearty breakfast she had devotions with me. She taught me to read and memorize Scripture and to pray. Mamma was not an educated woman academically or biblically. She knew a handful of precious Scriptures, which she had committed to memory. Two of them were Psalm 23 and the Lord's Prayer as recorded in Luke 11:1–4. As a sheep, I strayed far from the flock of the Good Shepherd. However, the mornings I spent with Mamma were well invested. I always remembered those two Scriptures. Many times when life's circumstances seemed overwhelming, I meditated on these passages, especially Psalm 23. I found myself walking down the street on more than one occasion not knowing where my next meal would come from, meditating on this powerful passage:

> The Lord is my shepherd, I shall not want. He maketh me to lie down in green pastures: he leadeth me beside the still waters. He restoreth my soul: he leadeth me in the paths of righteousness for his name's sake. Yea, though I walk through the valley of the shadow of death, I will fear no evil: for thou art with me; thy rod and thy staff they comfort me. Thou preparest a table before me in the presence of mine enemies: thou anointest my head with oil; my cup runneth over. Surely goodness and mercy shall follow me all the days of my life: and I will dwell in the house of the Lord for ever.

I am more grateful to my mother than words can express for taking the time to train me spiritually, especially for teaching me that very powerful passage of Scripture. I had no idea back then, though, how powerful it is. This brief but powerful portion of God's Word, hidden deep in the recesses of my sinful heart, would sustain me for many years as I lived away from the sheepfold, among the wolves.

For thirteen years I lived like a wolf. I lived among the wolves, while avoiding sheep like the plague. I did as the wolves did, while looking like a wolf. I talked like a wolf. I walked like a wolf. Anyone who saw me assumed I was a wolf. If ever I allowed myself to engage in deep thought for any length of time, I would realize I was not like the other wolves, though. Many things that wolves engaged in freely and enjoyed were repulsive to me. Certain things I learned to fake in order to convince my wolf peers that I was a wolf indeed.

Fortunately for me, there is a passage of Scripture in Matthew 18:12–14 that talks about the Good Shepherd. The Good Shepherd, it says, will leave ninety-nine sheep to go and search for one that is gone astray to bring him safely back into the fold. Though I had been successful in convincing many people for many years that I was a wolf, the plain truth was that I was a sheep. Not only was I a sheep, but I was a lost sheep at that. The biggest danger was that I didn't even know I was lost. Thankfully, I had a Good Shepherd who knew I was lost and would not rest until I was back in the fold. It took a while, but thanks to God's persistence with me, I made it back. Hallelujah!

I've had the occasion to share my personal testimony in many forums around the country. It's not uncommon, after I have talked about how God miraculously delivered me from a life of drugs and crime, for a parent to approach me. They tell me about their child, who they thought had made a sincere commitment to Jesus Christ as a youngster, but now his or her life bears no sign of that commitment. Some even tell me of children in prison that have switched from Christianity to Islam, the dominant movement for African-Americans in prison. I have looked into many a despair-filled face of a parent trying to make some sense of his adult children's lifestyles. They tell me how they have done their best to raise their children in the church. The parents had thought that their children were safe from the allurements of the world because of their childhood profession of Christ as Savior. Now they were left to wonder whether it had been a genuine profession. While I realize that children do sometimes make verbal confessions of Jesus Christ without truly understanding what their confessions mean, I try to help these hurting parents see this is not necessarily true in the case of their own adult children, now gone astray. It may be that the person made a genuine acceptance of Christ, even as I had done, yet for some reason decided it was more desirable to be a wolf than a sheep. If such were the case, they should be encouraged that their child may one day be returned to the fold by the Good Shepherd, just as I had been.

This book will distinguish itself from other books, such as *Cross and the Switchblade* and *If Jesus is the Answer What Are the Questions*, written about tough street guys who in the end surrendered their lives to Christ. Their stories can be summed up by the street poem which is a take-off of Psalm 23: Yeah though I walk through the valley of the shadow of death, I will fear no evil, because I'm the baddest so-and-so in the valley. On the contrary, I will report about how a guy who was not the baddest, the bravest, nor the brightest was protected from harm for many years in often hostile settings, by a loving and capable Shepherd. As a sheep, I was able to walk through the valley of the shadow of death only because He was with me, preserving my life. Without His tender care the real wolves would have ripped me from head to tail shortly after entering the valley. I would have made some wolf a tasty snack.

I'm certain there are many sheep out in the world garbed in wolf clothes. They can be found in many different walks of life—on street corners selling drugs, working in topless bars, in prison. Some can even be found in the business and professional arena.

It is my hope that this book will encourage those who pray daily for those lost sheep who are dear to them and inspire lost sheep to return to the fold, should it find its way into their hands.

Perhaps some are wondering how a sheep could survive in an

environment consisting mainly of wolves for thirteen years. This book, then, I pray, will serve to be a testimony of how God can keep His children, even the disobedient ones, in the most dangerous situations. It will show how He can, and will, deliver His children out of the most detestable lifestyles, and how He may even use them in some ways to His glory.

1

RUNAWAY CHILD RUNNING WILD

For good or ill, May 1968 is indelibly stamped in my memory. Detroit, Michigan, was still reeling from the wild, week-long period of civil protest characterized by looting, burning of neighborhood stores, snipers taking potshots at police and firemen, and streets patrolled by National Guardsmen in armored vehicles (the press referred to this calamitous week as the 1967 Riots). The intense turmoil had ended many months prior to my own crisis of faith, but still left were the physical scars: empty lots that had, a short time earlier, been home to thriving businesses; shells of burnt-out buildings; graffiti scrawled on the sides of buildings proclaiming popular riot rhetoric such as "Burn baby burn," "Off the pigs," "Black Power," and more. Those scars would remain far longer than anyone ever imagined. So would the resulting socioeconomic scars.

My own neighborhood was far from untouched by the riot. I was two and one-half years old when we moved there in 1955. Our family was only the second black family to move onto our block. At the time the area was heavily Jewish. It was not long after the blacks began to move in that the Jews began to move out. Looking back, it was amazing how fast the neighborhood transition took place. It was equally amazing how fast the neighborhood deteriorated.

My earlier memories of the neighborhood included majestic

trees and neatly manicured lawns. Homes were very well kept. The business streets were bustling with a thriving economy. On weekends one could always find crowds of people transacting business and buying goods. Business thrived in that area back then. However, very few were black owned. Many people were even employed within the neighborhood.

There were few reasons for a person to leave the neighborhood other than for work or social reasons. It was a time, as I remember, of neighborhoods and neighbors. Our family knew virtually every family within a five-block radius. It was like living in a small town. Everyone knew everyone else's business. Families were mostly two-parent households, in fact if not on paper. We knew where everyone worked, who worked and who didn't work. We knew which men would have to take to the alley when the welfare worker came into the neighborhood. We knew whose sons were in the military, in prison, and on drugs or alcohol. (Drugs, though, before 1968, were not a major factor in the neighborhood.)

We helped each other, back then, in the neighborhood. If one neighbor got their water shut off, they could depend on the neighbors to supply them with buckets of water. If someone's lights were cut off, we knew how to string an extension cord from the main line of another neighbor's house into the powerless neighbor's house, so that the family could enjoy electricity until they could have their power turned on. It would not be unusual for the neighborhood to play a major role in getting the needy neighbor's power turned on, or pay someone's rent.

We held each other accountable in the neighborhood in those days. It was not unusual to see one neighbor bawling out another neighbor's husband for being irresponsible in some way, such as infidelity, excessive drinking, or gambling. It was far from unusual to see a neighbor physically discipline children who were not theirs by blood. It was understood that if one of the neighbors saw me or my siblings misbehaving, it was their responsibility, not their option, to discipline us. My own father had no problem with the idea of community-oriented discipline. Because of his quickness to verbally reprimand and to physically chastise us, as well as other neighborhood children, he became known in the neighborhood as "Mr. Meany." I never remember another parent confronting my father because of his quickness to discipline other children.

Although the neighborhood was not as neat, nor as well kept as it had been when it was occupied by the Jews, or in the early days when the first families of blacks lived there, the neighbors still enjoyed a certain security. We, the neighbors, flourished in many ways. The neighborhood still produced hope in the hearts of parents and in the minds of children. The neighborhood was still a neighborhood.

Church buildings, preachers, and Christians were respected in the neighborhood, even by those who did not frequent the church. The pastor was usually the leader of his respective community. He was not only the spiritual leader, but often this role led him to become involved in the local school, community, and political matters. A prostitute wouldn't dream of soliciting a john in front of a church building. If a gang of men were shooting dice and drinking in a storefront and a group of church sisters walked past them, they would remove from sight the bottle and the dice, stand as they tipped their hats in respect, and say, "Pray for us all, sisters." Though there were few Catholics in the neighborhood, if a priest or a nun walked down the street, they received utmost respect and decorum.

It was extremely unusual for a person in the black community not to have some contact with the church. Most had, at some point in their lives, been regular attendees. Even among the criminal element in the community, there was a healthy respect for spiritual things, though they may not have understood them. It was considered taboo to steal from a church or to steal "in the Name of the Lord." The truculence of the sixties would change all this forever.

The month of May in southeast Michigan brings the most pleasant weather that one can imagine. Autumn is the only season that rivals spring in Michigan. In May the air is sweet with the fragrance of budding elm trees and blooming flowers. Temperatures range from being just cool enough to wear a light jacket to occasionally warm and sunny enough to sport a new pair of shorts. It is typically rainy in May, but the air is sweeter after a light spring shower.

May nights are especially pleasant. The temperatures are typically in the 60s. Those nights are known as "good sleeping weather." It was on such a night that I made a decision that would drastically change my life.

It was May 1968, when I was fifteen years old, the youngest of six children born to my parents who were both from rural Georgia. However, they did not know each other before coming to Detroit in the 30s. My father was totally illiterate. His mother had died shortly after he was born. Soon after that, his father left him with some relatives while he left Georgia, presumably to seek his fortune. He was raised by aunts and uncles until he was grown and moved to Detroit. Dad was forty-three years old before he saw his father again. That experience left him deeply hurt and resentful about life. My dad was a big man, about 6'2" and about 260 pounds. Besides a large potbelly, he consisted of all muscles. He had worked hard most of his life and was very strong. Because he always felt that he had gotten a raw deal out of life, he had a very quick temper. Often that temper would be unleashed on other men (white or black, it didn't matter to him), on my mother, and on us children. He was verbally abusive as well. His abusiveness drove all of his children away from him, most at premature ages. Although I know that my father believed in God and Jesus, he was never a church member.

My mother was strikingly beautiful in her prime—light complected, long black hair, beautiful hazel eyes, and shapely. However, by the time I was born, she was forty-two years old. Her hair was totally grey, and many of her teeth were missing. She had lost her youthful beauty and much of her self-esteem, although she was still a good-looking woman. Mamma was from an extremely poor family. Georgia sharecroppers were never considered high on the socio-economic scale.

Mamma often boasted about her seventh-grade education, the highest among her seven siblings. With a deep faith in Jesus, she took us all to church on Sundays, taught us Christian principles, and lived a life of love before us. It was her commitment to the Lord and to her family that kept us together in any fashion at all. She never allowed us to say a bad word about Dad in her presence. She

21

taught us to always stick together as a family.

Mamma had a daughter, Lillian, from a previous marriage. Lillian was much older than the rest of us, so it was hard to look on her as a sister. She never lived far from us, so we were in constant contact. Because Mamma married so young the first time (around thirteen years old) and had had a child at fourteen years of age, there is about a twenty-seven-year difference between my age and Lillian's. Lillian has children who are older than I. It wasn't seemly for children in those days to address adults by their first names, so we called her "Sister," until we were grown.

My oldest brother, Robert Jr., was the stern leader among the siblings. Quite big for his age (6'4" and 270 pounds when he was grown), he used his large frame to command respect from others, inside and outside the family. Feared in the neighborhood as a capable street fighter, he was called "Bam," short for Bambino, because of his similarity in build to the ever-popular Babe Ruth.

My next oldest brother, Isaac, was quite different from Bam—tall, but slender in build. He inherited my father's dark complexion and my mother's hair. He was quite handsome, a real lady's man as far back as I can remember. A very gifted artist in the making, unlike Bam, he detested violence.

Harold, the next oldest brother, was also tall, handsome, and very creative in his own right. Although he engaged in his share of mischief as a young boy, he was more the conformist of the family, not prone to get into serious trouble.

There was about a year's difference in age between Harold and my next oldest brother, Michael, or Mike as we called him. Shorter and stockier in build than all of us except Bam, Mike, it seems, was always in trouble for one thing or another. Before he was a teenager, he had earned a reputation as a rugged athlete and capable street fighter.

Next to Mike was Nadine, my sole sister by both parents. Because she was the only girl in the family, she was my father's pet. She also had a streak of tomboy in her. She got roughed up some, but we were all sworn to take care of her and protect her. Nadine was two years older than I, so we paired up. As we got older my father made us travel together. Although we naturally liked one another and enjoyed being together, this arrangement was sometimes embarrassing to both of us, especially as we became teenagers.

I was the last to be born to my parents. For a while I was neither tall nor short. Not at all athletic, I was a mediocre fighter. The thing that distinguished me from my siblings was that I was bright in school. Before I came along, no Williams had stood out academically. My mother hoped that I would one day become a doctor. I enjoyed school because that was the arena in which I could compete successfully. It is a truism that people generally enjoy what they excel in and excel in what they enjoy. School also became a refuge for me to escape the violence I experienced at home.

My father was a very austere man, very strict. I believe it had a lot to do with his being abandoned as an infant, and having to live with several different relatives. Because of his own unresolved inner pain he had developed a pattern of verbal and physical abuse not only toward the children, but also toward Mamma. Because of this violence in our home, a pattern began in which all of the children began to leave home at early ages.

Bam joined the army at the age of seventeen, after having run away several times and getting into several minor scrapes with the law. Several years after he got out of the army, he was sent to prison for armed robbery.

Isaac began to run away from home at the age of fourteen. Finally, at the age of nineteen, he left home and hitchhiked to Florida to live with some of Dad's relatives. He was killed at the age of nineteen by a jealous man for dating the man's estranged wife.

Harold lived at home until he was nineteen years old. Then he was drafted into the army where he spent most of his time stationed in what was then West Germany.

Mike began to run away from home around thirteen or fourteen years of age. When he was sixteen years old, he was arrested for armed robbery, tried as an adult, and sent to prison.

Nadine left home at the age of seventeen because she was afraid of what Dad's response would be to her pregnancy.

To cope with a terribly unstable home life, Mamma occasionally took solace from alcohol. She did not drink often, but she could not hold her liquor. She usually got drunk whenever she indulged. But perhaps that was her plan. When she drank, she had the unfortunate habit of challenging Dad. He was never the one to graciously respond to any kind of insult. We would beg her to keep quiet. Her classic response would be "I'm not afraid of him." I watched in horror on too many nights as Dad drove his massive, rough, black fist into the soft flesh of Mamma's fair-skinned face. The next morning she would be covered with dark blue and purple bruises all over her body. Often she attempted to leave, but where do middle-aged women with six children, with limited skills and education go to escape a familiar hell? You just stay and pray and pray and pray.

In short, my family life was not a pretty picture. By the time I was fifteen, Bam and Mike were in prison, Isaac was dead, Harold was in the military, and Nadine was pregnant out of wedlock. To top it off, because of Dad's failure to raise my older brothers, he clamped down on me even harder. He was determined, it seemed, not to let me go the same route, even if it killed me. He reminded me often that he would kill me if I didn't do what he said. I believed that he would do just that, especially during the frequent beatings I received. I became the object of class humor because I came to school with welts and bruises. One teacher snickered at me after he had called my father to report my classroom antics. Dad responded promptly by characteristically applying his old faithful razor strap to several tender parts of my anatomy rather indiscriminately.

By May 1968 I had grown weary of beatings and of being told how stupid and useless I was. I had grown tired of not being able to stay out at parties until a reasonable hour, like other kids my age. I had had it with having to run home from school because of my father's rule that if I lingered too long along the way, I got it, but good!

All of us—my brothers, my sister, and I—were raised in church. All of us had made a verbal commitment to the Lord Jesus Christ; yet my family was so devastated. Mamma taught me to read and to memorize Scripture regularly. I had heard many fiery sermons about how God had delivered Daniel from the lions, how He saved the three Hebrew boys, and how He gave David victory over the giant. The preacher promised that He would do the same for me. I prayed, oh how I prayed, that God would make a change in my family life. That He would make my father stop beating all of us. I prayed that my brothers would get out of prison. I even prayed that somehow it was a case of mistaken identity and that Isaac was not really dead. When none of those prayers were answered, I began to pray that God would kill Dad so that I could live a "normal" life.

Well, that didn't happen either. Little by little, I began to lose faith in what the preacher was saying. Did God really hear and answer prayers? Maybe God really did not exist—like some older boys had told me on the playground. Maybe I had been a sucker all those years for confessing Christ as my Lord and Savior, for spending all that time in Sunday school and church, and for believing that God was going to grant me my wishes if only I was a good little church boy.

By May 1968 Mike was a veteran convict in Ionia State Prison. He had earned the respect of his peers because he could take care of himself in prison. I imagine that he too had long since lost hope in a God who never stopped us from getting beaten. In prison he began to hear about a different kind of gospel ("good news"). It was the gospel of Elijah Muhammad. I had heard about Muhammad on the streets of the neighborhood, although I was not really attracted to him until Mike began to evangelize me. The older generation and those in the church had written him off as some kind of kook. I had also heard much about the new generation of Negro leaders, heroes and heroines, such as Malcolm X (who had recently been assassinated), Huey P. Newton, Bobby Seals, H. Rap Brown, and Angela Davis. All these folks had one thing in common: They all dismissed the church as socially irrelevant and a tool of the white man to keep black people down. Preachers, even Martin Luther King, were dismissed as Uncle Toms or pimps. Mike told me in his letters and on visits how Elijah Muhammad was going to change how black people were treated in this country. He was going to lead us into the Promised Land. There was no need praying to a "dead Jesus" who could not answer your prayers, even if He wanted to. If you want something, you are going to have to go out and fight for it, kill for it, or at least let the white man know that you are prepared to fight, kill, and die.

All of this began to sound very appealing to me. It seemed to make sense. We as a people didn't need religion; we needed liberation. It had become increasingly clear that religion was unable to help me. I needed liberation. So I turned my back on Christianity. I embraced Islam, although never wholeheartedly. Islam never really made sense to me, but the Mosque and the group identity provided what I needed for the moment, or so I thought. I still attended church because I had to, although I had become extremely cynical about Christianity.

I still recall that last whipping I received from Dad, in May of 1968. He accused me of misplacing a screwdriver that he had placed over the dining room door. I was not the one who moved it. He did not believe me. Although he could not prove that it was I who moved it, he wasted no time in administering swift punishment to me for something that I had no part in. By this time I had graduated from whipping to full-out beatings. He hit me, manhandled me, and verbally abused me. In a loud voice he told me that if I didn't like living there and did not want to obey his rules, I could leave.

As far back as I can remember, I was always one who became indignant at injustice. As I retired to my room, fingering my fresh set of welts and bruises, I felt that I had been dealt a terrible injustice. In my idealistic way of thinking, I believed that the victim of injustice would ultimately become a victor. This type of thinking prompted me to believe that whatever action I took in response to my unjust treatment would somehow succeed in remedying my situation. I began to make plans for action, or so I thought. Actually I was doing nothing more that following the program that had been set for me by my older brothers. I began to plan how I would run away from home.

The fact that I was planning to leave home came as no great revelation to Mamma. Mamma was in the basement washing clothes when I went to announce my great plan to her. "Mamma," I struggled to get the words out that I knew would hurt her deeply, "I'm leaving." Her efforts to talk me out of it were surprisingly weak. Frankly, I expected more. She looked so tired and exasperated when she turned her weatherworn, wrinkled face to me. She knew I would be stepping into a world I was totally unfamiliar with.

"Where you gon' go?" she asked, with years of agony furrowed across her forehead.

"I'm going to stay with Sister," I readily replied. "Sister told me that if I got tired of getting beat I could come and stay with her."

"How you gon' take care of yo'self?" she asked, wanting to believe I truly had some kind of real plan.

"I'm gonna work, Mamma. I'm gonna work and save my money." Tears were now streaming down my swollen face, stinging my bruises. "I'm gonna save my money and get us a place. I'm gonna come back and get you, Mamma, so he can't beat you no more either." I'm not sure that I ever believed these words as they came across my lips. What I really meant was that I could no longer stand to live in that atmosphere of constant terror. If Mamma was somehow trapped there, it was not a whole lot I could do to help her. I could not really look beyond my own hurt. It was every man and every woman for themselves.

Mamma knew that she could not stop me from leaving. She had lived that same scene four times before I played it. She had seen four other sons cross that threshold of no return to innocence. She had had her insides yanked out each time it happened. She rehearsed for me how Isaac had gotten killed in Florida. She reminded me of my two brothers in prison. She assured me that I knew nothing about human nature and the kinds of people I would encounter in the streets. "Promise me two thangs," she pleaded. "Promise me that you won't steal and you will stay in school."

"I promise, Mamma. I promise I won't steal and I won't drop out of school," I said, perhaps even believing that I could somehow keep that oath.

Nadine was sitting in her dimly lit bedroom getting ready for bed. "I'm leaving, Dedee," I told her. "I'm running away and going to stay with Sister." It was rather emotional leaving my sister to be

27

the last sibling in the house. However, Nadine was Dad's favorite, so she would be alright. She gave me what little change she had, barely enough to catch the bus to Sister's house, although Sister lived within walking distance, if one felt like walking. We said our good-byes and the escape plan was put into action.

Dad went to bed early as usual. After pretending to go to bed, I put my clothes back on and slipped out the back door. Creeping apprehensively down the back stairs, my heart was pounding so hard at the thought that Dad would hear me and give me a thrashing on top of the beating, that my ears ached. Finally, out the door! Fear caused the trip from the bedroom to the downstairs door seem like half an hour, though it must have taken only a minute or so.

It was a lovely May night. The air was so pleasant and refreshing to my violated skin. I closed the door quietly behind me, dashed across the backyard to the chain-link fence. Jumping the fence caused more noise to my sensitized ears than I thought possible. Then a terrifying thought occurred: What if Dad had heard the noise and was about to get after me? What if he had set me up and was planning to cut me off at the pass? Terror gripped my fifteen-year-old heart. I'd better run for it. Down the alley, almost stumbling and falling, remembering stories of how my older brothers had run away and how Dad had chased them. Dad had been quite an athlete in his day, and could still run pretty fast. He nearly caught Isaac once in a foot race, or so the story goes. Isaac was a much faster runner than I. The thought that Dad could chase me, and perhaps catch me, only intensified my anxiety.

When I made it to the end of the alley and out to the main street, I stopped running and began walking calmly in order not to look suspicious. There was no bus coming as I began walking toward Sister's house. A sense a freedom began to wash over this boy such as I had never experienced. Walking down Joy Road, 10:30 at night, by myself felt great. Looking into the faces of fifteen-year-olds today, it's hard to imagine one thinking that he can take care of himself on the streets of a major city at that age. Walking down that street with only the clothes on my back and bus fare in my pocket, having led a relatively sheltered life, with no previous exposure to street life, I was totally unprepared for the direction that my life was about to take. The things I would experience and see in the thirteen years that I would remain in the streets would scar my life in a way that many people cannot begin to imagine. The beatings I was about to receive from the streets over those years would make all of my father's beatings condensed into one moment feel like a mosquito bite.

No sooner than fifteen minutes after leaving home, I encountered my first test. I had decided to get off the main street and travel some side streets. A few blocks from the main street I encountered a group of six youths. Tales I had heard suggested that this could mean big trouble. My plan was to simply keep walking, ignoring the tough-looking boys. Maybe they would ignore me as well. Unfortunately, my hopes were not realized. As I approached them they called out to me from across the street. "Hey man, gimme a cigarette."

"I don't have one," I replied, trying not to appear as scared as I was.

Then came some words that chilled me to my toes. "Well, you better make one," one of the young men shouted as they started across the street. Was this some kind of sick cosmic joke? Could it be true that I was running away because of being beaten only to experience a beating at the hands of street thugs? Now, this was the point at which a fast runner would have taken his leave. However, I was not a fast runner. I figured that if I ran they would likely catch me, and then I would really be in trouble. Whatever was to happen, I would have to take my chances at talking my way out of a potentially painful situation. Pain on top of pain did not appeal to me at all.

By now the six of them were standing right in front of me. Definitely the hoodlum type, most of them wore "do rags" on their processed heads. I recognized a couple of them from Sister's neighborhood as resident gangbangers. This revelation caused a lump in my throat and my limbs to tremble. I must remain cool, though, I thought.

"So why don't you have no cigarette?" Barry, obviously the

leader, challenged.

At this point he was right in my face. A good answer was a must. "I'm a Muslim, brother," I blurted out before I knew it. "As Salaam Alaikum," I continued.

"Oh yeah, you a Mooslim, man, that's cool," said Barry, nodding to his companions that I was not to be harmed. They had all been coiled as if ready to pounce on me if I had given the wrong answer or made the wrong move. Now they were relaxed. Their body language said I was alright with them. Then, even the gangbangers had an abiding respect for the Black Muslims. Malcolm X was a Muslim. Many young men from the neighborhood that went to prison came back as Black Muslims. There was and continues to be a very strong Islamic movement in the prisons.

"Where you on yo' way to, blood?" Barry asked.

I told them that I was on my way to my sister's house. They not only allowed me to pass unharmed, but also told me to use their names if I was stopped by anyone else on the way. I couldn't believe that I had gotten through that ordeal unscathed, all because I told them I was a Muslim. That experience would cause me to cling to the idea of passing myself off as a Muslim for longer than I might have under different circumstances, even though I never subscribed to very many Islamic tenets.

Finally, Sister's house was in view. Sister's husband Arthur greeted me at the door. Arthur was about fourteen or fifteen years older than Sister, which made him about the same age as Mamma. It was strange to think of him as my brother-in-law. He could have passed for my grandfather. His eyes could not believe what they saw when he knew that it was me at the door at that time of night. He was even more shocked after he let me in and saw all the bruises on my arms and face. I told him and Sister what had happened and asked them if I could stay with them. Sister said that I could. She sent me to bed in the basement with my nephew, Kenny, who was my age. As sleep finally began to take control, Arthur and Sister could be heard engaging in a heated discussion behind their bedroom door.

I sat at the breakfast table the next morning with sister's children, Kenny, Catherine, Lillian Ann, and Sandra (her youngest,

Michelle would be born in yet a few years; her oldest, Jesse was nearly ten years my senior). I was told by Sister that I could stay with her family indefinitely. Her only terms were that I must continue to go to school, even that day, bruises and all. No one can imagine the delight that news brought to me. Sister's children were around my age. I had always envied them. They all had bikes. I never owned one, although we could easily have afforded one. They were generally allowed to do more fun things than my siblings and I. I had always had a ball when we went there to visit; now I was going to be able to live there. Excited about my newfound freedom, trying to ignore my wounds, hoping that they were invisible to others, I went to school. The pitied and confused looks I received proved they were not. Still I was nervous, thinking that Dad could burst into the classroom at any moment and drag me out. I knew that I would get the beating of my life if that happened. I was embarrassed as my fellow students looked on my bruises and discretely turned away so as not to cause me further shame. Although I had obeyed Sister by going to school, my mind was preoccupied. My teachers tried to act as if there was nothing unusual.

It was hard for me to grasp the fact that I had really done it. There are certain things that seem to be inevitable—manifest destiny is what they used to call it. Running away from Dad was one of those things. In my own way I had finally defied him. I could not imagine what my life would be like now.

As nerve-wracking as it was to attend school constantly entertaining the thought that Dad could always find me there, I had to keep going. After all, there was the promise to Mamma and the edict of Sister that I continue to attend school. The source of those fears never came to pass. Dad never came looking for me. He never tried to make contact of any kind with me. I found out later that he had called the police the day after I ran away. Mamma told me that they asked him if he knew where I was. He said that he did. They then, very rudely, advised him to go and get me himself. It seems as though my parent's address had been put on that precinct's trouble list. As it was, whenever there was an inordinate amount of police calls to a particular house in a precinct, the desk sergeant was slow, even reluctant, to send officers out on a call to that address.

Ours had become such a house because of all the calls over the years. They were called when Dad beat Mamma. They were called whenever one of us ran away. They were called when Dad had a beef with the tenants in our two-family flat (we rented out the downstairs). They were called even for very simple reasons, such as someone parking across our driveway. The Tenth Precinct police were not very excited about responding to a call at 8921 Otsego.

As it turned out, there was never any pressure from Dad for me to return home. After a time I even became confident enough to go to the house to visit Mamma. The fact that Dad did not try to get me to come home was a tremendous relief from the standpoint that I was hunted by neither him nor the police. But his lack of interest in pursuing me also had its negative effects. It made me feel that the reason he did not try to get me to come back home was that he did not want me. That thought would nag me for years to come, often stinging my soul worse than any beating had stung my flesh.

Nadine ran away about two weeks after I had. She was pregnant and afraid of what Dad's response would be. He had warned her from time to time that if she ever got pregnant out of wedlock, it would be bad news for her. Although he never spelled out what that bad news might entail, Nadine (or Dedee, as we called her) was not inclined to stick around and find out exactly what he meant. Therefore, two weeks after I showed up at Sister's house, Dedee also showed up needing refuge from Dad's wrath. When Dad found out that she was pregnant, he did not fall into a fit of rage as everyone had expected. He sought her out to assure her that she could return home without fear of punishment. He would drive to Sister's house where we both lived, pick her up in his car, and take her for a short drive trying to convince her that it was alright to come back home. Although I was happy that Dedee had this option open to her, the fact that he tried to get her to come back home and virtually ignored me played havoc with what little self-esteem I had left.

After I had been away from home for about six weeks, having successfully completed tenth grade, things seemed to be going quite well. Free from my dad's tyranny, I didn't have to worry about when my next beating would come. I had grown an Afro hairstyle, something that I was unable to do at home.

My life was about to take a drastic turn, though. I could never forget the devastating feeling that washed over me the day that Sister told me that she was no longer able to allow me to live with her. I would have to go back home, she told me. GO BACK HOME! This was something I dreaded from the beginning, that I would ever have to go back home. What would Dad's reaction be? Surely I would receive a beating for having left home in the first place. Things, I feared, would be worse for me than ever before. Being the only child in the home meant also being the only object of Dad's rage. I shuddered at the thought, but sister assured me that I could not remain there. With Dedee and me both living there, she told me, it was too much strain on their family finances and on her marriage. It had not occurred to me that I should have been working in order to help out financially. I thought that I could live as other fifteen-year-olds, even as my nephew, Kenny. I was not like other fifteen-year-olds, though. I was a runaway. Dedee's boyfriend, Richard, was in his late twenties and was helping her out financially, so the choice was easy; she could stay, I had to go back home.

I packed my bags with all the enthusiasm of a man on his way to the electric chair. Dad had allowed me to retrieve all of my belongings shortly after I left home. Mamma had given me an old, beat-up suitcase that we had in the attic. I agonized with every garment I folded into that old suitcase. The walk back to my parents' home seemed at least twice as long as the walk to Sister's.

In those days, gangbangers were not all that plentiful during daylight hours. So I felt comfortable as I walked. Dumbarton Street was lined with large apartment buildings. At one time it had been quite an exclusive street to live on. Now, though, it seemed more like a housing project. Many families and individuals just up from the South and other parts of the country, seeking employment in one of the auto factories, lived in these buildings. There was a good number of street people, pimps, thieves, stick-up men, and prostitutes who lived in those buildings, as well as many hardworking families and individuals who were trying to survive. Richard, Dedee's boyfriend, lived in one of those buildings. He fit into at least two of the aforementioned categories: He had come from Springfield, Ohio, to work in an auto factory. He also had an extensive background as a street person. Dumbarton was two blocks from my parents' home. I was just about to round the corner that would take me back home, racking my brain all the while, trying to think of some option other than going back home, when I heard a familiar voice. "Hey Bro Joe," Richard called out to me from in front of his building. He called me "Bro Joe" because of my claiming to be a Black Muslim. They addressed each other as "brother" and "sister." Richard also claimed to be a Black Muslim, although neither of us really followed the religion's tenets, except for not eating pork. Although I made feeble claims toward Islam for only two years, this nickname would stick with me for life. Because of our interest in the Islamic faith, we became somewhat close over the weeks that he had visited with Dedee at Sister's house. I began to really look up to him. He seemed to always have money. He dressed flashy and projected himself as being well abreast of the ways of the streets. Such ways were somewhat intriguing to me. Richard was a substance abuser. Although early in our acquaintance he only allowed me to see him smoke weed (marijuana) and drink wine, the range of the substances he used was much greater.

"Hey, man, where you goin' wit' such a long face?" he chided and smiled. I was glad to see a friendly face and to have the opportunity to pause awhile before making the final leg of my short journey. "I gotta go home," I told him with my shoulders slumped and feeling drained of energy. "Sister told me that I couldn't stay with her no more. I gotta go back home, but I know my old man is gonna kill me. I know it."

"Come on down to my crib (home). I got an apartment in the basement here," he said, gesturing toward a brown brick building. "I got some pluck (wine); let's rap for a while."

It was gratifying to have an older male taking an interest in me. It had been a while since I had had the companionship of an older brother. I was not an athlete, so I didn't have the benefit of having a coach as a mentor. It was refreshing to think about going to Richard's apartment to compose myself before going back home.

"Rich, man, this is a sharp crib," I shouted as he opened the door before me. Actually, it was a very simple basement apartment, rather sparsely furnished. Rich had a stereo player sitting by the window and a color television. To me, this was all the comfort a young man could hope for.

We sat for a while sipping cheap wine and listening to jazz. After about an hour or so of talking, Rich looked up at me and said with a grin, "Bro Joe, you don't have to go home if you don't want to. You can stay here with me." I could hardly believe he said that to me. It was totally unexpected, beyond my wildest dreams. To be able to live in a "cool" apartment with an older male whom I looked up to was an extremely exciting prospect, especially when the alternative was considered. I said "yeah" without asking any questions, without probing the reasoning behind Rich's generous offer. All I could think about was that I was again saved from Dad. Little did I know then, but life would never be the same.

Ironically, in my first year on the streets the Temptations came out with a song called "Runaway Child" that almost perfectly summed up my situation. Some of the song's lyrics that were continually repeated were: *Runaway child runnin' wild, runnin' wild—you better go back home, where you belong.* But going back home meant suffering mental and physical abuse. I could not take the advice of what was then my favorite singing group.

2

A PROMISE BROKEN

I t was good to be back in the old neighborhood again. I liked living with Rich better than living with Sister. Rich was cool and had many cool friends. There was no curfew, and I could even have friends over to visit. It was summer and life was buzzing in the neighborhood. I could look out the window and see just who was playing basketball on the playground across the street.

My day consisted of hanging out on the playground, although I did not have enough confidence to play basketball with the others because I was not a good athlete. So, naturally, anyone who wanted to win would not pick me to be on their team. Even if one of my brothers picked me to try to boost my confidence, the others would complain when I fumbled the ball or failed to contribute to the team's victory. My all-around self-confidence was so low by now that I was not about to ask to be on a team or try to call a turn and pick a team of my own. So I sat or stood by the fence, watched the others play, and talked to my friends when they were not playing. I would have given anything or done anything to feel like I was accepted by the others.

In the summer of 1968, many of us youngsters began to experiment with soft drugs (marijuana and wine). I had already begun to drink cheap, light wine with my nephew Kenny while at

Sister's house. Although Rich never encouraged me to smoke marijuana, it was always around the house. He and his friends smoked it freely as I sat with them and drank beer and wine. Curious, I tried my first joint (marijuana cigarette) at a party that summer. All the kids there were my age and had a little experience with cheap wine. I had purchased some marijuana from one of the dealers in the neighborhood and bought some skins (cigarette papers) at the store. Carl, a friend from school, and I pretended that we were veteran weed smokers. Neither of us knew how to roll the cigarettes, so more weed fell out of the papers than we smoked. We also pretended that we were high.

After Rich found out that I had smoked weed, he allowed me to smoke with him. One warm afternoon I sat listening to jazz, drinking beer, and smoking weed with Rich and the next door neighbor. This was my first time ever really inhaling it. I got so high that I could not thread the tape onto the take-up reel on Rich's reel-to-reel tape recorder. This ridiculous event was in no way funny. Yet it tickled me so much that I sprawled out on the floor laughing so hard that it frightened the next-door neighbor. He got up and left, thinking that I had lost my mind. Rich helped me into the bed and I lay there with the ceiling spinning. I was totally out of control. They say M.J. is not addictive. I am here to tell you that I became totally hooked on weed from that time on. I needed to feel good, and marijuana gave me the good feeling I was looking for. I had no idea what a great price I would later pay for what I saw then as a harmless pursuit.

That summer, weed would become my best friend. I soon learned how to roll joints that looked like store-bought cigarettes. Even though I could not play basketball, football, or baseball with my peers, most of us had begun to smoke weed. I had found a common ground on which to interact with my friends. Since I could roll so well, my company was welcome—I had discovered a contribution I could make.

We smoked weed on the playground, in the apartment, in friends' basements, and at parties. Weed was in. It was abundant. It was cheap. You could buy a deuce pack for two dollars and smoke for a couple of days, perhaps; or you could purchase a joint for fifty cents and smoke for a large portion of the day. Even though I was only fifteen years old, I could, in essence, obtain illegal drugs easier than I could obtain beer and wine.

Also, weed became my best friend because I had become very shy at times, especially around girls. After smoking about half a joint and drinking some wine or beer, I would loosen up a bit and become more sociable. Marijuana served to elevate my poor self-image somewhat, by making me feel that I was cool when I smoked it. Also, since there were many girls who smoked, possessing marijuana made one's company more appealing.

In the fall of 1968, only a few months after I had left home, I broke one of the promises I made to Mamma. I began to steal. There was a group of boys in the neighborhood who were noted as accomplished thieves. They often boasted of their exploits of stealing from department stores and breaking into cars. They would often flash the money they had amassed from their craft. One day on the playground, the leader of that group of boys asked me to hang out with them. Flattered to be asked to socialize with a group of streetwise youth, I gladly consented. It was shortly after this that I began going out with them on weekends to "rip off tape decks" (break into cars, and steal the eight-track tape decks).

I had gotten a taste of working that summer with some other neighborhood youths at a temporary employment service. We acquired false identification cards to push our ages up to eighteen so that we could enter the workforce as adults. I worked at a steel mill, cold storage warehouses, as a general laborer, and at other menial jobs for $10 per day. This was the beginning of my work experience. My early coworkers were winos and transients who had failed to make it into the regular workforce. This was not a very inspiring start, to say the least.

In the fall I could not even consider working a temporary labor job because of school. Working in the car wash proved to be in many ways more exhausting than the worst temporary jobs I ever had and paid even less. It was not even guaranteed that when one showed up at the car wash in the morning he could work. It depended upon the weather and how many men got there before you did. Yet I needed money. Unfortunately, I did not spend enough time trying to come up with a creative, legal solution.

In an attempt to solve my money problems, I began to go out with this group of boys to receive on-the-job training in ripping off tape decks. Martin, the leader of the group, had been on the streets for many years, although he was only sixteen years old. He looked as if he were at least five years older than the rest of us. This older facade was partially due to his long processed hair, or "do" as we called it. Martin lived with his grandmother. He and his two brothers and one sister called her "Granny." Granny seemed as if she was ancient. Their mother had died years earlier. They didn't know who their father was. Martin's older brother Juan was a big man and street tough. He ran a local weed house. He and his partner Jimmy allowed us to cop (buy) weed from them. Martin's only sister, Janie, was about nineteen years old. A beautiful young woman, she loved to dress up and go out to parties with her boyfriend, Clyde. His brother, Prophet, was about twelve years old. He had a lovely first tenor voice and loved to sit on the front porch singing Temptations' songs.

Granny was too old and tired to keep up with Martin. A troubled young man, at sixteen he was already an alcoholic with an extensive juvenile record for crimes including car theft, breaking and entering, and assault. He had already been in several juvenile institutions. A very angry person, he would regularly get into fights, even with friends.

Greg, the youngest member of the gang, was Martin's protégé. Fourteen years old, he was already an accomplished thief. He had not had the hard home life that Martin had had but chose the streets as a way of life for himself. His father was away working a great deal of the time. His mother was mentally ill and not able to offer Greg and his older brother any structure.

Eddie was the other regular member of the group. He was a medium-height, muscular-built fifteen-year-old who seemed somewhat mentally slow. He didn't have much input into the group's activities but always went along with the crowd.

I knew less about the streets than any of the others. Because of this, I was easily taken advantage of, having been raised with a sense of fairness. In the streets, however, whatever you could get away with was considered fair. I had been taught that people should look out for each other. In the streets, one only had to look out for himself. In fact, if one did not look out for himself, it was assured that no one would look out for him. Because it took me so long to learn and assimilate the street mind-set, I only received a small fraction of the value of the goods I stole. This gullibility was, no doubt, the very reason I was invited to be a part of the group.

Every weekend night—rain, snow, or flood—we were at our job of ripping off tape decks. Our favorite place to victimize was at the Grande Ballroom. The Grande was a concert hall for hippies. Although by this time the neighborhood was nearly all black, every weekend white hippies would pour in from the suburbs and Canada (Windsor, Ontario, was just across the Detroit River) to listen to hard rock bands and get high on drugs. Every weekend we would be there to welcome them to the neighborhood by breaking into their cars.

We used a neighborhood dopeman by the name of "Boo" to fence our stolen goods. A fence buys stolen merchandise and resells it for a profit. In the black community, as a matter of fact, drug dealers are the most likely fences. They have direct access to the thieves who are normally drug users of some sort. Boo had an apartment over a storefront on Grand River Avenue. I had heard about his legendary dope-house for some time before I was allowed to go there. I was intrigued to no end at the thought of going to a dope-house where many of the area players—pimps, prostitutes, con men, boosters (thieves), and worse—hung out and partied. I simply could not wait until I could frequent Boo's.

One night we netted a choice haul of stolen goods. That night I was allowed to go to Boo's along with Martin and Greg to sell the loot. I was truly excited about the prospect; it was like a rite of passage. It meant that I was passing from one grade to another. Think of it! Little old me rubbing shoulders with the "big time" street players.

The apartment was just as I had imagined. The inside in no way matched the outside. It was lavishly furnished. Boo had the finest color television and stereo that anyone in this neighborhood had ever seen. There were pimps decked out in fine clothes resplendent with sparkling diamonds and gold. Prostitutes draped both arms, wearing seductive clothing, painted faces, and glamour wigs. Jazz sizzled softly in the background as players of every craft transacted business and socialized over their drug of choice. Boo was a short, broad man, dark skinned with deep lines in his face. His scarred and scary demeanor suggested that he had experienced much in the streets. Sharply dressed, he was not about to allow himself to be outdone by the others when it came to flashy, expensive jewelry. He darted in and out of the front room as he transacted business with all in the apartment.

Boo had two French poodles that roamed freely throughout the apartment. They seemed as if they did not belong in such a setting. It was explained to me, though, that Boo had specially trained these dogs to perform various sexual acts with some of the women who frequented his dope-house. These were generally women who were addicted to drugs and for some reason were not able to pay or perhaps had past-due drug bills. Boo would use these acts to entertain himself and his clients.

While I sat there with Martin and Greg, in awe of all that went on around me, a homosexual came into the room and seated himself close to me and my fellows. Now, I had been in the presence of homosexuals before and after that, but this guy was extremely unattractive. He was as ugly as a baboon sucking on a lemon. He had very rough skin. The whites of his eyes were tinted yellow. I found this guy to be quite amusing just to look at. He turned to me and my friends and said in a voice that he tried to make sound feminine, but only succeeded in sounding absurd, "Hi fellas." I had been smoking weed the entire time. When he said "Hi," I fell into a fit of laughter. Again, like in Rich's apartment, I totally lost it. Laughter rattled through my slim frame so hard that everyone in the place was now eyeing me. I could not stop laughing. The homosexual was thoroughly embarrassed. He was much bigger than I. He probably could have very easily beaten me to death had he wanted. Thankfully, he was disposed to be a lady that night. Boo was infuriated. He threw me out at once. "Get this silly nigger outta my joint, and don't never bring him back in here!" he shouted to Martin. Martin and Greg dragged me out of the apartment by the elbows. I could see the fear and surprise in their faces. I should have been afraid for my life, but I was too delirious to be afraid. That was the first and only opportunity I had to visit Boo's.

Since Dad worked the day shift at Ford Motor Company, it was usually safe for me to visit Mamma during the daytime while he was at work. Dad had the reputation for hardly missing a day of work, not even for illness. It was usually a rather safe bet that I could visit just about every day if I wanted to. Mamma encouraged these visits. She always wanted to know that I was alright. If she saw me regularly, she felt better. She also made it her job to make sure that I got a decent meal—at least occasionally. When I left home, I had been chubby. Five to six weeks later I had lost all my excess weight and even became quite slim. Over the first summer that I was away from home, I also began to grow taller. It seems that I grew at least four inches during those few months. This added growth contributed to my looking too skinny for Mamma's liking. Her feeling that I was not eating properly was based on fact. Because of my times of famine, I was always happy to receive that feast that Mamma would lay out for me whenever I visited her. I found out that Dad had also given her instructions to feed me well whenever I came by.

In the late fall I stopped by to pay my respects to Mamma's kitchen. As I walked through the gate and headed for the steps, I noticed that there was something amiss. The steps were covered with blood. I was overwhelmed with a feeling of horror. As I went up the stairs I saw Dad's lunch pail lying on the steps. It was bent and bloody. "Oh, Lord, no!" I cried out. "What has he done to my Mamma now?" I asked myself, afraid of what the answer might be. I rang the doorbell frantically. I pounded on the door but got no answer. I never considered any other explanation for what I beheld other than my father had beaten my mother worse than ever before, and she was lying in some cold emergency room, if she was indeed alive. After all, he had beaten her bloody on so many occasions before.

After failing to gain entry to the house, I ran out the gate and through the alley to Martin's house. "This is the last time that he will ever beat my mother," I convinced myself. "He's got to die; I've got to kill him to free Mamma from him." I devised a hasty plan in my head concerning how I would murder Dad. The only place that I knew for sure that I could get my hands on a gun was from Dad himself. I knew exactly where he kept his guns. All I had to do was break into the house, steal one of his guns, and lay in wait outside the house before he left for work, spring from behind the bushes, and gun him down. I believed that I could pull it off and get away with it. The only problem was that I had never broken into a house before on my own. I needed some help. I knew that Martin knew how.

Martin was not even out of the bed when I entered his bedroom. "Get up!" I shouted to him. "I need you to help me do something." Martin listened to me intently as I explained to him that Dad had beaten Mamma for the last time and that I intended to kill Dad. "Help me break into the house," I explained to him. "You can keep everything else; I just want the guns." At the thought of loot, Martin sprang from the bed and put on his clothes. He grabbed his coat without even washing his face and was out the door. First we stopped by Greg's house to enlist his help. Then the three of us went to work.

We broke into the house through the basement window. We found a hatchet in a cabinet in the outside hallway, the same hallway I had months earlier used as an escape route, and chopped through the back door that led to the kitchen. Once inside the house, Martin and Greg went wild loading up loot. I was aghast to see even more blood inside the house. I was even more determined to carry out my plan. We axed through the locked closet that I knew contained the guns. That closet was filled with all kinds of loot, but for the life of me I could not find the guns I sought. Finally, we decided that we should make our getaway before the police came. I was forced to leave without the item I came for, leaving my parents' home in shambles.

I returned to the apartment later that evening. When it got darker outside we would go to fence the loot. As I entered the door I was met by Dedee. She had moved in with Rich about a month earlier. I could see that she was excited about something. "Did you hear about what happened?" she asked in a troubled voice. "Yeah, I know what happened, that fat mother beat up Mamma again. But don't worry, I'm going to kill his   ," I assured her.

"What are you talking about?" Dedee asked with a confused look on her face. "Dad was in an accident this morning," she continued. "His car is a total wreck. He's still in the hospital." I slumped down into the poorly padded chair in the living room of the apartment, feeling as low as the underside of a slug. How could I have jumped to such a conclusion? My parents' home had been practically destroyed on a mistaken assumption. There was no way that I could think of to rectify this wrong. How could it be made right again? We could not simply return the stolen goods, even if Martin and Greg would go along with that idea, which I didn't believe they would. If Dad wasn't dead and he found out that it was I who had wrecked and looted his house, my behind would be grass and he was going to be the lawn mower.

Slowly, sadly, with trembling lips and shaky voice I explained to Rich and Dedee what I had done. They both sat on the sofa with a look of shock on their faces. They couldn't believe how stupid I was. They didn't know what to say. After being bawled out by both of them, I rejoined my troupe. They couldn't care less about my dilemma. All they wanted was to fence the hot goods. I decided to take the small share of the stolen goods they offered me and try to forget the stupid blunder I had made, hoping to God that Dad never found out.

After dark we decided to make our move to sell our ill-gotten goods. We took the usual route to Boo's place. I was loaded down with my share of the take. We had to cross Grand River to get to our destination. Grand River is a large street that always has a lot of traffic. We seemed to make it across alright one more time. Martin and Greg went into the back door to Boo's while I waited for them to come back to get my stuff to take in, since I was forever banned from Boo's due to my outburst of laughter. As I was waiting in the alley, I noticed a set of headlights turn into the alley. "Oh Lord, I hope that is not the police," I thought. I would rather get caught breaking into Fort Knox than to get caught with Dad's stolen property. I was certain that the latter carried the death penalty.

My worst fears were realized when the car got closer and I could distinguish the faces of the two white men in plain clothing, driving a black Plymouth. This was definitely the police. They stopped the car about twenty yards from where I was standing. Both doors opened. Two rather large men got out at the same time. One officer shined a flashlight into my eyes, all but blinding me. "Come over here!" he shouted to me.

Right, I thought to myself, and with the immortal words of Stephan Fletcher speaking directly to my pedal extremities, I declared, "Feet, don't fail me now." And with that I decided to make a foot race of it. I turned the corner of the alley at breakneck speed and headed for Grand River. *If I can just make it across Grand River I will make it,* I thought. On the other side of Grand River I knew every alley, the peculiar turn of every street, and which yards had dogs in them. *If I can make it across the River, I know I will get away,* I reasoned. I approached Grand River in full stride. Though I am not usually a fast runner, Jessie Owens would have been envious of my form that night. I was picking them up and putting them down, as the saying goes. Pop! A shot rang out behind me. If I needed any added incentive, this was it. There were cars, buses, and trucks whizzing up and down that busy thoroughfare as I reached the curb. I was too frightened to even slow down. I kept right on going in full stride, hoping that I wouldn't get flattened by a bus. In the traffic at least, I figured, I had a chance of survival. Should I stop and give up, the infamous Detroit Police might kill me, or worse, they might turn over my remains to Dad and he would kill me again.

Miraculously, before I realized it, I was on the other side of the street. Through the alley I flew, over one fence, across a side street, through another yard, down another alley, never looking behind me. I ran until my lungs felt like they would explode. Completely exhausted, I expected the police to catch up to me at any moment; that moment, fortunately for me, never arrived.

I went home completely defeated. First, I had made the terrible blunder of breaking into my parents' home. Now, I had absolutely nothing to show for it.

It was not uncommon for us to run across small quantities of marijuana, alcohol, and other drugs while breaking into cars. One Sunday night as we worked at our chosen craft, we found some weed and a bottle of Southern Comfort whiskey. We sat on Martin's top porch and quickly consumed both. Martin, our fearless leader, asked after we were all fairly intoxicated from the dangerous mixture, "What y'all wanna do tonight?"

Someone answered, "Let's rip off a ride (car)." So we went out in search of a car to steal, armed with only our "key to the city" (a screwdriver).

Only a few blocks away we found what we were searching for: an old Chevy. These cars were known for being particularly easy to steal. All it required was for one to stick the large screwdriver between the front and rear windows and to pop the lock up. Once inside, Martin skillfully stuck the screwdriver into the ignition switch. He then gripped the screwdriver handle with a pair of pliers. He twisted the screwdriver with all his might, breaking the ignition switch, and allowing the screwdriver to serve as a key. Another turn of the screwdriver and the old Chevy was started. We joyfully pulled out from the curb with drunken Martin at the wheel.

"Well, where do y'all wanna go to," slurred Martin to the rest of us. I was in the front passenger's seat. Greg and Eddie were in the rear seat.

"Let's go down on 12th Street," I blurted out. For some time I had wanted to frequent this famous street in the evening. This street between Joy Road and West Grand Boulevard was legendary in Detroit. It was the place where all the hustlers, all the players in the entire city hung out. The lights were bright on 12th Street.

Famous pimps and players from all across the country were known to frequent 12th Street. Wild stories about the crazy happenings on the fabled stretch of asphalt and concrete had been told on many a street corner and playground. I just had to see it for myself.

"Yeah," the others agreed, "let's go down on 12th Street."

We made a couple of turns and proceeded east on Joy Road, heading toward our destination. I could only imagine what excitement would greet us after we arrived. I could picture men dressed to kill standing back in storefront doorways within hollering distance of their stable of women dressed in shimmering miniskirts and high-heeled shoes. I could envision the fine cars that would cruise up and down the street. For some reason, Martin decided to get off the street and drive down some alleys. Down one alley we went, then another, as I dreamed about the excitement that lay ahead of us and how we would be able to go back to the neighborhood and brag (perhaps lie) about the good time we had had on 12th Street. Suddenly, bright lights blinded us from the front. Red flashing lights flooded the alley. My ears were deafened by the screaming siren.

"The pigs!" somebody screamed in terror. Martin slammed on the brakes of the clunky Chevy and swerved into a garage as the car came to a stop.

"Run," somebody else advised. Martin was so drunk that as he opened his door in an attempt to escape, he fell out and simply lay there. I leaped from my seat and headed for a nearby fence to jump, and to hopefully out maneuver the police if I could not outrun them. As I hit the fence, on my way to freedom, I thought, I was instead grasped by the strong hands of one of the officers. In an instant, I was yanked from the fence and slammed against the garage. In fact, none of us was successful in getting more than a few steps away from the car before we were caught by the obviously very experienced officers.

They piled us all in the backseat of their patrol car and handcuffed us. Martin was only half-conscious. Greg leaned over and whispered to Eddie and me that it was a certainty that Martin would be returned to the Juvenile facility until he was eighteen, because he was on probation. Greg and Eddie also had Juvenile records. Greg pleaded with me to say that I was the driver of the car, also the one who initially stole it. His rationale was simple and streetwise. Since I did not have a record, the authorities would only give me a slap on the wrist. The others faced the possibility of spending time in lockup. I quickly agreed to take the rap. We were promptly hauled off to the police station.

This was my first time experiencing the inside of a police station, except for helping Dad fill out an accident report. Unfortunately, it would not be my last. The Tenth Precinct police station was noted for being one of the roughest in the city. I had heard many a story of young neighborhood men being brutalized in that place. I had two very powerful emotions attempting to dominate my mind. Competing with the fear of the unknown was a sense of pride because I was passing through another important rite of passage in my street culture. It was unusual for a man in my culture not to have been at least as far as the police station, if not also to the county jail or even the state prison.

Our experience at the police station did not last very long. None of us received any violent treatment at the hands of the officers. We were processed as juveniles and quickly transported to the Wayne County Youth Home. Contrary to what one might expect, this encounter with the juvenile officials was to be more scary than the arrest and police station experience. As we were piled into the police car to be transported to the youth home, the stories began of the horrors that take place at that facility. The seasoned veterans hit me with a barrage of tales of boys being beaten by youth workers. I was sickened by stories of how bad the food would be. It was frightening to hear accounts of boys perpetrating acts of violence against one another. It quickly became apparent to me that my companions were veterans and that I was a novice to this experience. As a rookie I could expect to be tested more than the rest. I was frightened, but tried not to let on.

Arriving at the youth home, we were taken to a room where we were strip-searched. Our personal clothing and belongings were taken from us. We were given an issue of institutional clothing that

48

was either too big or too small. We were taken into a large open room that served as a gym under less crowded circumstances, but now served as a dormitory. We were given thin mattresses and assigned a place on the floor. We hardly got any sleep that night. There were as many as forty boys in the gym sharing our accommodations. Once during the night, a boy who had effeminate characteristics got up to go to the restroom. Soon after, another boy followed him into the restroom. The next morning, Martin claimed that both boys were homosexuals and that they had committed a sex act in the restroom.

We were roused early the next morning for breakfast. The staff threatened to beat us if we left any food on our plates. It was a real effort for me to force down the bland oatmeal and half-ripe banana, but facing the consequences of not eating the food gave me the incentive I needed to clean my plate.

When I was arrested and questioned about my family, there was no way I was going to give the authorities my parents' names, address, and phone number. I had told them that my parents lived in Georgia and that I lived with my sister. I depended on Dedee to verify my story and simply to come and spring me, no questions asked. I found out, though, on my way to my hearing the next day after our arrest, that she had completely blown my cover. Not only had she not gone along with my lie, but she promptly informed Mamma that I had been arrested and brought her to the youth home to sit in on my hearing.

The youth workers escorted me by way of an elevator from the gym to the hearing room. It was from them that I first learned that my cover had been blown. "So your parents are in Georgia, are they?" one of them asked wryly as he swung his key chain made of plastic lace. These men were known for whipping the boys with these key chains. "Well, it just so happens that your mother and sister are waiting for you downstairs." Suddenly I was filled with emotion. First, I fully expected to get my behind whipped right there on that elevator for lying. Then, I realized how heartbroken Mamma would be seeing me in this state. I had hoped that she would not find out about this episode of my life, ever. I broke into tears. Mamma had made me promise that I would not steal. I had lied to her for months, assuring her that I was keeping my promise. Now I was found out and about to get beaten on top of it.

To my surprise, the youth worker had pity on me and did not whip me during this longest elevator ride I had ever experienced (although it only involved a few floors). We went to the hearing room where Mamma and Dedee sat and listened in disappointment as I admitted to being the one who stole the car. The referee had an idea that I was covering for Martin and gave me an opportunity to change my story, but I stuck to my guns. Just as Greg had said, I was only given a warning and released to Mamma and Dedee. On the way back up on the elevator my escorts threatened me. If I ever came back to the youth home for any crime, they would whip me for sure. I decided at that point that if I was ever arrested again, even if I was still a juvenile, that I would tell the police that I was an adult to avoid going back to the youth home. I had no intention of giving up my lifestyle of crime, however. The rhythm of the streets had gotten into my blood. It would take another thirteen years for this disease to run its course.

Martin's hearing was later in the day. He was released later than the rest of us. Upon our release we were not certain that our tactic had worked completely. We were fearful that the referee had not bought my story and had simply remanded Martin to the custody of the state. When Martin got out, however, Greg and Eddie promptly came by the apartment to pick me up. We went to Martin's house with great joy and expectation of a happy reunion.

We were greeted at the door by a very somber Martin, one that I had never seen before. After we were seated in the living room, Granny shuffled into the room. She stopped in front of me and pointed a crooked finger in my face. "You little skinny nigger," she began her verbal assault upon me. "I knew you were a sneaky little weasel when I first met you. You been comin' roun' here trying to act so nice and polite, and all the time you been doin' all kinds of dirt. You done went out and got dis here boy (pointing to an angelic looking Martin) in trouble, and he done almost had to go back to da home. I hate you!" she shouted at me. All the time I was looking at Martin, waiting for him to come to my defense. I knew that at any moment he was going to explain to Granny that she had it all wrong, that I had actually saved him from being institutionalized by taking the rap for him, and at risk to myself. I'm a hero, after all. . . but Martin only dropped his head. He was satisfied to allow me to bear the full brunt of Granny's anger. He never said a word. The others sat around nervously as Granny showed me to the door, letting me know in no uncertain terms that I was no longer welcome in her home.

I never got to see 12th Street in its glory days, not that night or any other night. That was the area where the '67 riot had broken out. It had been badly damaged by fire and vandalism during that time of unrest. Little did I know then, but 12th Street was already slated for the wrecking ball, to be replaced with low-income housing and a strip mall. So ended my dreams of hanging out on 12th Street with the street players. So also ended my close association with Martin, Greg, and Eddie. My criminal career was far from being over, however. Quite the contrary. Shortly I would experience an episode that I shall never forget, one that shall forever scar my soul.

3

DEATH OF INNOCENCE

Gunshots, screams of pain, blood-soaked snow, and total confusion are memories that dominate my recollection of the winter of 1968–69. Every young person must entertain dreams of graduation day. Every parent hopes and prays that this dream will be realized in the life of his child. No one, though, wants or expects that graduation will include events that will irrevocably assassinate the innocent youth of his child.

The fall of 1968 had come and gone. Eight months earlier an innocent child had ventured onto the streets of an unforgiving city. Eight months crammed with raw experiences, sharp disappointments, conflicting values, and exhilarating experiences had turned a shy youngster into a cynical street tough. Ugly lessons about human nature had been learned. Weaknesses in my own character had been brought to the forefront in the face of "push come to shove."

That fall I went from being an honor roll student to a knuckle-head, playing hooky with the neighborhood hoodlums, filling my gut with cheap wine instead of nourishment, my brain with marijuana instead of precious knowledge. For the first time in my life, I experienced academic failure. For the first time in my life, I didn't care. Being "book smart" was not something that went over big with people who made their living on the streets. After all, most of them found their way to the street because they had met with failure in school and other social institutions.

That fall brought with it the introduction of my new acquaintance masquerading as a friend. That fall I began to flirt with one that later became the love of my life. This pretend friend made me feel better than I had felt in all my life. From this pretend friend I received courage and strength when I would have shrank in cowardice. A feeling of power and assurance was present whenever we got together. One who would have normally been terribly shy became bold and confident, even aggressive. This pretend friend, in truth, was not a friend to me or anyone else. In fact, such an association almost always left its victims in the end robbed of self-respect, years of productivity, and any shreds of dignity they might have otherwise amassed, or dead.

Kirk Adams was the leader of a bunch of young criminals many times more desperate than my former associates. He was fourteen years old when we began what turned out to be a tragic association. He was by far the biggest fourteen-year-old I had ever met. His face was not the face of a child, but the face of a man with too many bad memories. A six-foot frame added to his older appearance. The thick mass of processed hair on his head added further to this delusion which he nurtured and enjoyed. His eyes revealed hurt, shame, and a deep need to be loved. This could not be hidden with drugs or rage, though he tried.

Though this young man was two years my junior, he had experienced more pain and hardship than many will experience in an entire lifetime. He was the product of teenage parents. His mother openly resented his birth and told him so. His being born "messed up" her life. She married Kirk's father to give her baby a name. Their marriage relationship was stormy and short-lived. Out of this relationship were born two other boys.

With the breakup of the marriage, Mrs. Adams found herself in the unenviable position of trying to raise three boys in a rough neighborhood, alone. She worked the afternoon shift at a hospital. That meant that Kirk and his younger brothers were left on their own while their mother attempted to provide for them as best as she could.

Hubert Brown (we called him U-bone) was a year younger than me. He also had lived more of the underside of life than I could have imagined at that time. U-bone was average height, wiry of build with sharp facial features, and dark brown-skinned. We had known each other for about five years. There was never any depth to our association before this point, though. I'm sure that his having the reputation of being an extremely troubled child had a lot to do with it. As a preadolescent, he would roam aimlessly through the neighborhood shooting other children, small animals, birds, any target he could find with his slingshot. He was even insolent with Dad, which was rare. So Dad could not stand the sight of him, even as a child.

Receiving the curse of Granny left me in need of finding someone to hang out with. Tragically, I chose this deadly bunch. Both of these young men were heroin addicts. Even though I had observed Rich and his friends snorting (inhaling) heroin (blow, scag, boy, jive, white horse, pee, raw), I had never attempted to experiment with it myself. Rich had warned me to stick with the weed and wine. Secretly, though, the desire was there to try a little blow. A little urging from Kirk and U-bone helped to intensify the urge to try something with a little more kick.

With the exception of my own parents' house, I had never broken into a home. This practice, though, was the stock-in-trade of Kirk and U-bone. The revenue gained by breaking into a few cars over the weekend could not satisfy the monkeys on their backs (heroin habits). They needed a hustle that would provide more money, regular money. B&E was just the hustle that could provide the needed income.

"Come on, Joe man, We gon' show you how to make some real money," Kirk offered. "Breakin' into cars is fo' babies," he continued. "You can hang out with us and hustle with us." Again, poor self-esteem prevailed. I was flattered to be asked. *Wow! After having been on the street only a few months, look at me now, running with the big dogs,* I thought.

Every sundown found us on the prowl. Each night meant that someone's home would be violated. Some unsuspecting family would come home to a broken-in door, possessions strewn about their home, all their valuables gone. Color TVs were hot items, easy to get rid of. Stereos were almost as easy to fence. Jewelry was sure to bring a fast exchange of either drugs or cash. Guns meant instant money. We weren't that picky though. Clothes, lamps, wall hangings, we took whatever we could get.

Juan, Martin's older brother, was a favorite fence for my new associates. Juan was a heavy-set young man of about twenty-one years old. He was as hard as the life he had experienced as a youngster. He gave the impression that he cared for no one but himself. The finer things he had missed out on growing up poor would never allude him again. No one would stop him. The expensive clothes that draped his large frame testified to that. The diamonds on his fingers cried out, "Amen!"

Along with his partner Jimmy, Juan ran a dope-house only one block from my parents' home. It was apparent that Juan was the leader of the two. They had some of the best weed in the neighborhood. Going to Juan to sell the loot and purchase weed was a reward worth stealing for, worth waiting for. It was Juan who formally introduced me to my long-time pretend friend, Mr. H.

Breaking into houses was hard work. Or so it seemed. One consumed a great deal of energy. Adrenaline pumped fiercely during the course of the act. So many things could go wrong. The police could be called. In those days they would actually respond. The occupants could return home. There might be a large, well-trained attack dog on the premises. A person could get arrested, bitten, beaten, or even killed attempting to rob someone's home.

So after a hard evening's work, we always looked forward to going to Juan's. This night was different though. This night was life changing. "Hey, Juan, man, you got some of that baaad weed?" I questioned as I rested in the plush crushed velvet sofa. "Man, yo' reefer is always the bomb."

"Naw young blood, ain't you heard? There's a panic on weed. I can't get nothing," Juan assured me. "Man, I got some boss scag, though. You oughta try some," he offered, shaking a vile of white powder in my face.

A panic is when a certain type of product is nearly impossible to be found. In this instance, the marijuana had been dried up. Theory has it that in 1968, the year after the riot, heroin was dumped onto the streets of the ghettos across America. Although heroin had been in existence since around the turn of the century, it never was a real factor in the ghetto until 1968. Whether heroin became superabundant that year in order to quiet the increasingly outspoken black population as is suggested by some who hold to this theory, or whether it just happened to become more prevalent that year, no one would argue that this drug had a devastating impact on the black community.

"Naw man, I don't mess with nothing but weed," I replied. Disappointment would hardly describe the feelings of this fifteen-year-old marijuana addict. How long would this panic last? How could I find a way to enjoy the pleasure of my good friend, Mary Jane? What would I do for my high now that there was no weed anywhere in town? Remembering how peaceful and cool Rich and his friends became began to weaken my resistance to the crude sales tactics of Juan. After all, peace was what my searching was all about. What a bargain! Some people spend their entire lives and never find peace. Juan was offering me the peace I had been seeking for only one dollar bill.

I contemplated the pile of white powder on the Temptations album cover on the coffee table in front of me. This powder had become a god to my associates. They often extolled its virtues to me. "Man, that reefer just make you silly. You need to try some of dis scag, Joe man," Kirk often advised me. "This stuff is what you need if you really want to feel good." I truly did want to feel good. Good was a feeling that had very often alluded me up to that point in my life. "Sniff, sniff."

Someone was calling me from a distant place. The voice was so familiar. I could not respond. The motion of my limbs defied me. It was Rich's voice. I wanted to respond, but something was preventing me. Finally, I slowly emerged from a fog into the light. Why was

Rich so frantically slapping me? When I came to my senses, I realized that I was on the back steps of the apartment building we lived in. Rich had me by my bony shoulders shaking me. Every time he released me, my head fell between my legs. Slowly, with Rich's help, I began to gain control of my body. Standing was not easy, but I managed. My stomach began to churn like never before. In an instant, everything I had eaten and drunk that day was on the black rubber runner that lined the apartment floor. I felt so bad, yet I felt so good.

The penny cap I had snorted kept me high all that night and all the next day. It was an experience that I found absolutely unique, strangely pleasurable. Heroin gives a person a false feeling of being in control. No fear can creep into the heart inhabited by "King Heroin." The person whose veins flow with this evil drug, no matter how usually timid, suddenly possesses nerves of steel. A remedy for all of my insecurities was now just a short walk away, just a dollar away, just a snort away. I was falling in love. Mary Jane had to make way for a newfound friend. She would one day be totally replaced by him. For Heroin is a jealous friend. He will not share affection with another for long.

Just a few months prior, Sunday morning would have found me attentively sitting in Sunday school and church. Those days were simply a scorned memory now. I lay on the living room sofa as the bells of St. Theresa Catholic Church reminded the residents of the neighborhood of our sins of the night before. It's not unusual in the wintertime in Detroit for the sun to hide from view for months. Winter days were typically cold, gray, icy, depressing affairs. Such was the day that would rob me of my innocence forever.

"Joe, it's me, Kirk," a voice claimed from outside the living room window of the apartment. I raised up slowly to see Kirk's large brown face peering into the room. "Come on, man, I got a sweet thing for us," Kirk promised. "I know where there is a house that's got a color TV, jewelry, money, and all kinds of stuff, and the people are in church, so come on 'cause we got to hurry." I had slept in my clothes that night, so I simply needed to put on my shoes and comb my Afro. I borrowed Rich's white trench coat as I headed out the door to meet Kirk. Kirk wore a long tweed coat that day. By the time I got outside, U-bone had arrived on the scene.

We walked for a little over a mile through the southern portion of the neighborhood and then down Grand River toward downtown. The location of this particular proposed robbery site was farther than we had ever ventured up until now; however, no one questioned how we would cart the loot back to the neighborhood. For some time we had planned to get out of the B&E business and go into the drug-dealing business. We had been stockpiling stolen goods in an abandoned apartment building for several weeks. Supposedly, Kirk was holding on to some cash we had earned selling stolen goods. Our plan was to save our money to get an apartment and an initial stash of drugs. We figured that all we needed was a good start, and we could be rich in no time selling drugs. This break-in was to be the one to put us over the top.

After a brisk walk of over a half an hour we arrived at a neighborhood that was completely foreign to me. This neighborhood was even older than the one I grew up in. Unlike my own neighborhood, there were no brick houses, only wood frame, one- and two-family homes. We finally arrived at the house we were to break into. It was an old two-family flat with a separate outdoor entrance to the first floor off a back porch. This back door would be our entry into the house. According to Kirk, no one was supposed to be home. We were totally unsophisticated in our approach to gaining entry into homes. Usually we carried a pry bar to pry the door open or a large screwdriver to wedge between the door and the jamb. If that didn't work, we simply kicked the door in.

Kirk wedged his large frame between the back door and a beam that supported the upstairs porch. He pressed his thick shoulder hard against the back door. We could tell that the door was beginning to give a little. Kirk began to bounce his weight against the door. "What y'all standin' there fo'?" he grunted. "Help me, pusssh!" U-bone and I joined in with our partner in crime. The door was no match for three desperate junkies. Crack! The door sprung open. However, to our dismay, there was a night chain holding the door from opening all the way, preventing our entrance.

U-bone and I were shocked to see a frail, hunched-over figure rush toward the door. "Kirk, thought nobody wasn't home, man," U-bone protested. "Man, les get outta here," I pleaded. "What y'all want?" the old man whined. "I ain't got nothin'. Please, go on an' leave me alone." "Kirk, les go man," U-bone urged in agreement with me. "Y'all scared of that old man?" Kirk scolded in an attempt to shame us. "We can handle him. We'll just push him out of the way," he continued. Kirk and the old man were engaged in a tug-of-war with the badly splintered door. Then Kirk uttered what he must have thought was a stroke of genius at the time. "We're the police. We looking for John Johnson. Get out of the way!" Kirk shouted in the old man's face. U-bone and I looked at each other in exasperation. Kirk was absolutely determined by hook or crook to gain entry into this man's home and rob him of his valuables. We both gave in, knowing that if we didn't help Kirk with his mission, we would be scorned and laughed at as being weak and scared, frightened by a little old man, no less. We helped him to push the door the rest of the way in.

Once we were inside, the old man quickly retreated to another room, all the while pleading with us to leave his humble dwelling. Kirk would occasionally shout to him to be quiet and stay out of the way if he didn't want to get hurt. Kirk and U-bone had been in the street long enough to know that they could not trust each other. They had been breaking into homes long enough to know where the real valuables were. Both of them quickly located what they must have taken to be the master bedroom. Kirk instructed me to check out the rest of the house while he and U-bone worked the bedroom. From the living room where I scrounged for anything worth stealing, I could hear them gleefully rummaging through the items in the bedroom.

Suddenly, the situation changed. As if something had snapped inside the old man, turning him from a sniveling, cowering, help-less victim, his voice and demeanor were transformed. I whirled around from where I was to see what could have caused such a change. I turned to see the old man standing in the doorway of the room he had retreated into extending two pistols. "Put that stuff down and come out of there, or I'll shoot," he demanded. One of the guns was so big that he appeared to have difficulty holding it steady. Cries of fears began pouring from the bedroom. "Please, don't shoot. We give up," U-bone pleaded. "Don't shoot us; oh please don't shoot us," Kirk cried.

The man's peripheral vision had to be non-existent. I was standing merely a few feet away from him with nothing between us. He had to but turn forty-five degrees and I was a dead man. Quickly, I ducked behind the living room wall. The front door was but a few feet away. Could I reach it in time, before the old man heard me moving and shot me? There seemed to be twenty locks and chains on that door. Turn this one, slide the chain off of this one. I was making too much noise. He must hear me. Will I make it out with my life? I could still hear Kirk and U-bone pleading as I opened the front door. To my surprise, there was an elderly woman standing in the doorway when I opened the door. I could tell that my presence shocked her. She, however, was no more shocked and traumatized than I. I didn't know what else to do, so I brushed past her on my way out and muttered something like, "Good morning, ma'am."

Finally, I was outside! A feeling of relief washed over me momentarily. *But I cannot leave my friends in this predicament. I must do something,* I thought, but what could I do? I decided to go to the side window and crash a brick through it to distract the old man, then Kirk and U-bone would have a few seconds to make their escape. The brick I sought was lying handily by the front porch. I rushed to the window of the room the man was standing in, realizing that I could still get shot as a result of my actions. I drew my arm back to hurl the brick. Then, "crack, crack," the shots rang out. Screams of horror and pain filled the air. Glass began to shatter, a rumbling sound came from within the house. All of a sudden Kirk burst through the back door, leaping from the porch with a suitcase in his hand. *What a sight, what a relief! He's alright,* I thought. Shots again rang out, "crack, crack, crack." Kirk attempted to hurdle a wooden fence that led to the side street. The force of the bullet slamming into his body drove him instead right into the fence. The fence collapsed with a loud crunch under his weight.

At that moment, I had been rushing out to meet him unaware that he was in the sight of the old man's pistol. As he went down, Kirk saw me. I ran out to pick him up, with no regard to being in the line of fire. "Help me, Joe," he managed to utter. His limp body felt as if it weighed five hundred pounds as I dragged him out of the line of fire and onto the curb of the side street. His breathing was heavy and labored, his eyes shut tight. "I'm shot, I'm shot," he continually cried.

Unlike in the movies, there was no puddle of blood on the ground. As a matter of fact, there was no blood. Frantically, I searched to locate my friend's wounds, as if I could do something for him. I could find no evidence of wounds through his thick tweed coat, only a small burn hole that looked like a cigarette burn. He must not have gotten shot after all. He must have heard the shots and been scared so bad that he thought he was shot. "Git up, Kirk," I urged him. "Man, you ain't shot, I can't find no bullet holes in you. Git up, man." Why did he insist he was shot when there was no evidence, no blood on the snowy ground or on his coat or on my hand, no blood? "I'm shot, man, I need help," he insisted. "Call the police," he pleaded with me. In those days there was no Emergency Medical Service. The police handled these kinds of calls. They had long black station wagons especially suited for these occasions. "Call the police?" I questioned Kirk's reasoning. Calling the police would mean that he would surely go to jail. But the choice was obvious to this veteran of the streets. Jail was preferable to hell.

The closest house was but a few steps away. "Lady, there's a man that's been shot at the side of your house. Call the police," I instructed the woman of the house. "How you know he's been shot?" she nervously replied. "I saw him get shot," I answered. "Lady, please call the police, hurry up."

Running back to where Kirk lay, it was quite apparent that his condition was worsening. His breaths grew short and shallow. "Hang on, brother the police is on the way," I assured him. By now a crowd had begun to gather. While holding Kirk in my arms, he breathed deep and hard and then stopped breathing. I thought I felt his breathing start back. Now I could hear the sirens. The crowd grew even larger. I felt it best that I melt back into the crowd. Perhaps no one (especially the police) would know that I was with Kirk.

The long black station wagon eased down the slushy side street, parting the crowd. I watched as they slid Kirk's long body into the back of the wagon. With sirens blaring, the dark chariot faded from sight. It was as if I had become invisible. No one saw me standing there with mud and ice on Rich's beautiful white trench coat—not the crowd, not the police. Slowly, I turned from the crowd and began my journey back to the neighborhood. All during the walk home my mind played back the scene of Kirk's body giving way to the force of the bullets that felled him. It was like a hideous instant replay constantly playing inside my head. I hoped against hope, though, that everything would somehow work out alright, but how could it? *Yea, though I walk through the valley of the shadow of death . . .*

I had no idea about how U-bone had fared through this frenzy of activity which included shattered glass, shouts of terror, gunshots, the smell of gun smoke, and masks of horror in the foreign neighborhood. Where was he? Was he dead? Had he too gotten shot by the old man, the victim turned victor? Hopefully, he had gotten away and could shed some light on what happened inside the house.

It was strange going to school the next day after having aged so many years only the day before. My peers had no idea of the kind of creature in their midst who was not like them at all. They had no clue as to how they should interpret the sudden hollowness of my hazel-brown eyes, the slump of my slim shoulders. As soon as my classes were finished for the day, I would head straight for U-bone's house to see what the deal was.

U-bone opened the door possessing an unusually wild expression on his face. He knew a secret that he had no intention of sharing with me, perhaps with no other living soul ever—a secret too dark and shameful to ever tell.

"Man, what happened in there? You know Kirk got shot. Leas' I think he got shot. He thought he was shot, but I didn't see no

62

blood, man. What happened?" I rambled to U-bone. U-bone did not go to school. He must have sat home all of Sunday evening and all of Monday constructing his story. He may have had several elaborate accounts of what happened inside the house—none of which would have been true. "We were in the bedroom loading up the stuff in an old suitcase we found under the bed when the old man hollered at us from the other room," U-bone began. "When we turned around we saw he was holding two guns in his hands. He said that he would kill us if we didn't come out and give up. We jumped behind the wall where he could not see us—Kirk looked at me and said 'U-bone, you go ahead out of the window. I'll stay here and try to keep him busy while you get away.' I jumped out of the window and kept running. I heard some shots, but I didn't know what was happenin'; I just kept runnin'."

Had he not been a prolific thief, U-bone could have easily made a living as a fiction writer or an actor. I figure that when the old man came out of the room with the guns, the law of self-preservation must have prevailed in the hearts of these two veteran street survivalists. There must have been a race and a struggle to see who could get out of the window first. U-bone obviously won the race or the struggle. Kirk then decided his best chance was to go back out the way he came in. He must have used his street savvy to get out of many a tight spot in his brief tenure on the street. This was not a spot that he would successfully get out of. He was shot once with the .22 caliber handgun as he ran out the door. A .38 caliber bullet caught him in the back as he attempted to jump the wooden fence.

Not knowing where Kirk was nor his condition, U-bone and I began calling the local lock-ups in an attempt to locate him. We began with lock-ups, because not seeing the pool of blood I would have expected to see in the case of a gunshot wound, I still hoped that Kirk had not actually been shot, but perhaps scared witless. We searched for Kirk using his real name and his alias, Anthony Green. No luck! There was no Kirk Adams nor Anthony Green imprisoned in any facility we contacted. Next, we decided to call the hospitals that accepted gunshot wounds. There was no patient by the name of Kirk Adams nor Anthony Green. Finally, we surrendered to the idea of checking the city morgue for our companion.

"Wayne County Medical Examiner," the female voice on the other end of the line uttered matter-of-factly. "Hello," I managed. "Do you have a gunshot victim by the name of Kirk Adams?"

"No, we do not have a Kirk Adams," the voice answered. A moment of relief washed over me temporarily. "Do you have an Anthony Green?" I forced myself to question. "Yes, we have Anthony Green, a black male, six feet, 180 pounds."

A feeling of sickness and fear attacked me, pervading every inch of my body. Numbly I hung up the phone. U-bone was no psychic, but he did a good job of reading my mind. "He's dead, ain't he?" U-bone shouted in terror, grabbing my elbow. "Yeah, he dead man; Kirk is dead," I assured him.

For a while we sat staring at each other, totally paralyzed by the horror of the moment. All of the saliva instantly evaporated from my mouth. My stomach flipped unceasingly. My mind was caught in a whirlpool of devastating consequences. How could this be? After all, we were invincible. We were too young to die. One is not here one day and just gone the next. Or is he?

Circumstances did not allow us to ponder our painful questions for long. We knew that we were the only ones in the world who knew this horrific secret. The medical examiner thought she had the body of a twenty-one-year-old Anthony Green in their freezer. Only U-bone and I knew that it was actually the remains of a fourteen-year-old Kirk Adams. The most frightening question begged an answer. Who would relay this news to Kirk's mother?

Neither of us could muster the courage nor integrity needed to perform this dreaded duty. We decided to let the medical examiner discover Kirk's identity on her own. Mrs. Adams would have to hear it from someone else. Besides, the dread of seeing Mrs. Adams's face when she found out that her eldest son was taken from her by the ever-violent street life was too hard to consider.

Days passed as we guarded our grievous secret. Days had

passed and Mrs. Adams still had not been notified by the medical examiner. After not hearing from Kirk for several days, his mother began to suspect that all was not well. When she began to ask around the neighborhood as to where Kirk might be or what might have happened to him, the trail led back to me.

After the shooting, I stayed close to the house, hoping not to receive a visit from the police or Mrs. Adams. But on the following Tuesday, Martin and Greg paid me a visit. Mrs. Adams had asked them to investigate Kirk's disappearance. Reluctantly, I revisited the details of the terrible day for Martin and Greg. Indignant that I had not come forth with the information on my own, they insisted I tell my story to Mrs. Adams.

Mrs. Adams took the news with all the grief, hysteria, and anger I had feared. Much of her anger was directed at me. Why had I survived while her son perished? This was a point that I could not sympathize with her on.

A day later when U-bone was questioned by the neighborhood council of thieves, he wove a tale that I found unrecognizable. According to his story, he was a hero who offered his own life up for his dear friend Kirk. Also, in his story, I was portrayed as a cowardly fiend that ran away when the action got too hot. U-bone told all who would listen that I ran out on the two of them at the first sign of danger. Interestingly, no one questioned why I was around to pull Kirk out of the line of fire. No one raised the question of how I was there to comfort my friend and call for help for him, if I had run away from the scene as U-bone suggested.

Thanks to U-bone's lying attempt to salvage his own miserable image in the youthful criminal community, I became a scourge among my deviant peers. No gang of thieves would consider including me in their circle. There were only two people alive who knew the truth. No one was listening to me, and U-bone was not about to relate a truth that would reveal his own cowardice and treacherous character.

So far failure had been the only thing I was consistent at in my attempt to survive on the streets. The mystique of street life had alluded my every attempt at realizing it. Misery had followed me from the home of my parents and seemed determined not to allow my escape, ever.

4

IF A BULLFROG HAD WHEELS

No blow the streets could have possibly dealt could compare to the realization that Mamma had found out about the shooting incident. Mysteriously, she had a way of finding out about all the shameful endeavors I participated in during my tenure on the streets. The despair she must have felt knowing that another of her children had been so close to death must have been unbearable. Mamma began to put pressure on Nadine to make me come back home.

After being assured that it was no longer possible for me to live with them, Nadine and Rich suggested that I go back home. I would have rather lived in an alley with the rats as my fellow tenants than to return to the horror of the Williams household. However, with no one to hustle with, with no means of support, facing one of the coldest winters I can remember, I decided to give "home" another chance. Mamma assured me that things would be better this time. Life at home would not be so bad this time. I would see that she was right.

After Kirk's death, I experienced a time of spiritual and psychological crisis. I thought that I should have been shattered emotionally because of what I had been through. Surprisingly, I felt very little emotionally. Had the streets had such a dramatic effect on my soul so soon? This was a shame that could not be shared with others. It had to be kept inside.

Lanard Braxton was a friend I had known almost all my life. The Braxtons lived around the corner from my parents' home. I found them to be a delightful and amusing family. They had migrated from Tennessee to Detroit in the early '50s. In Tennessee, the family worked as sharecroppers on a backwoods plantation near Mississippi. The story was that Daddy Braxton got into some kind of trouble with the other sharecroppers. Sanctions the family suffered caused them to move to Detroit in search of a better life.

The Braxtons were a family that lived well below the poverty line. However, they had a love for life that I have witnessed in few families of any social status. They loved to drink whiskey, gamble, and party on weekends. Occasionally, Mamma Braxton, or Frankie as she was known to the adults, attended a nearby Baptist church.

Going back home did not turn out to be such a good idea. Dad seemed resentful that I had dared to defy his laws by my initial escape. He was determined to let me know that he was still king of his domain and that I was yet a peasant. One night I came in later than Dad had instructed me to.

Lanard had broken his foot while playing basketball at a neighborhood gym. I helped him to get back home by allowing him to put most of his weight on my shoulder. The Braxtons did not own an automobile, so Mamma Braxton asked me to go to the clinic with Lanard in a taxicab. By the time the cast was placed on Lanard's foot and I was able to get him back home, I was past my curfew.

When I entered the house, I was very unpleasantly surprised to find Dad standing behind the door with a broomstick. "Nigga, didn't I tell you to be in dis house by nine o'clock?" he roared, waving the thick stick wildly. "I ought to wear you out wit' dis stick," he threatened.

"But Dad," I defended, "Lanard broke his foot and I had to take him to the hospital." I pleaded, "Please, don't hit me."

"Boy, don't you think you can come and go in this house any time you please," he shouted. "You been out there in dem streets livin' wild and think you can bring dat stuff in here, you cain't," he assured me. "Thangs ain't changed none since you been gone."

Surprisingly, he turned and walked into his bedroom without beating me with his club. I fully expected to be beaten bloody with that stick. Nevertheless, as Dad had so pointedly stated, things had not changed. Living under the threat of physical violence was no more appealing than it had been a year before. It was time to leave. But how could I break my mother's heart again?

Now it was spring. The winter chill had retreated in the face of warm breezes and budding branches. *This time I can make it,* I thought. I had to make it.

Appealing to the parents of my friend Lanard for temporary shelter seemed like a reasonable way in which to proceed. Allowing someone to live under their roof was nothing new to this most gracious family. In fact, they had done it many times in the past. Taking someone into one's home, especially a young person, was not a strange custom in the black community back in those days. The practice is not unheard of today. Few people in the neighborhood had food to spare. Yet there were few that would refuse a meal to a hungry soul. The Braxton family were true believers in this religion of hospitality.

I was informally adopted by this family after Mamma and Daddy Braxton learned of my plight, my tragic home life. As mentioned above, Dad's reputation for being an extremely harsh disciplinarian had spread throughout the neighborhood. He was not totally unknown to the Braxton clan. They assured me that I could stay as long as I needed to. I rejoiced at my renewed freedom from potential physical and constant emotional abuse. The process of informal adoption was a common practice in the black community that obviously had its roots on the plantations of the south. Many children, mostly kin, were taken in and raised by families other than their own. No one went to court to formalize the process. The agreement was not entered into with any thought of compensation from any outside agency. It was merely an arrangement of love.

The Braxton family income consisted of a meager welfare grant. Daddy Braxton was a functional illiterate. He was never able to acquire a steady job, perhaps because of his limited education. His binge alcoholism certainly did not serve as an asset to his finding and maintaining gainful employment. He did, however, perform whatever odd jobs around the neighborhood he could find.

Although there seemed to always be a lack of money in the Braxton house, there was always enough to share with others. The family found an interesting way of supplementing their income.

Mamma Braxton was a very heavy, medium brown-skinned woman about the same age as my own Mamma. She also had born children past the age of forty. She was so heavy that she appeared to rock from side to side, her limp cotton housedress swaying wide-ly with every step as she walked. Her extra weight was no doubt a result of a combination of her having born thirteen children and her plantation-style, high-fat diet. During times when there was quiet in the house, having brief moments to reflect back over her hard life, she mourned the death of her six children who died in childbirth and a seventh one who died as a child. She had lost many children between the birth of Lanard and his next oldest brother. For this reason, she nurtured a special affection for Lanard. He was her "baby."

Mamma Braxton had done something that was extremely rare for her generation. She had at least made it to high school, if she hadn't indeed graduated. Her wisdom and understanding of life far exceeded anything she ever learned in a classroom, though. From her I learned the meaning of mother-wit. In her way she was immensely wise. She was famous for her sayings. One of her say-ings I was particularly fond of was "If a bullfrog had wheels, he wouldn't bump his behind; he would just roll on." She used this saying when she caught one of us lingering too long in the world of fantasy, the world of "if." This family provided many very vital respites for me during my early years of learning how to survive in the mean streets of Detroit. The relationship between Lanard and me deepened from one of mere friendship to that of brothers. His grown siblings began to view me as a member of the family.

Living with the Braxtons meant that I would have support in continuing my education. All of the Braxton male children had dropped out of school before they graduated. Lanard was Mamma Braxton's last and best hope that she would produce a male high school graduate. Lanard and I had been in the same classroom in junior high. He was a bright student who was popular with all the teachers and students, especially the girls. Mamma Braxton was going to hear nothing about him entertaining the idea of dropping out of high school. This meant that as long as I remained a part of the Braxton household, school was also a high priority for me in her eyes. So far, I was at least able to keep this part of the promise I had made to my own mamma.

Gambling became a part of my experience as a direct result of becoming a Williams-Braxton. This was the trademark of the family. It was a source of family income. Mamma Braxton belonged to a gambling club. This club consisted of mostly women who hosted gambling games in their homes on a certain Friday of the month. People from all over the city came to participate in these all-night gambling fests. Blackjack was king at these parties. It was not unusual, though, for a mean game of poker or Tunk to take place as well.

On the Friday that Mamma Braxton's turn to host the game rolled around, the excitement began to build early. At least a week ahead of time, Lanard would begin to make known to his mother what his most pressing financial needs were. No matter what happened, she would make sure that the game met these needs. As the host, she would cut the card games. It was not unusual on a good night (especially around the first of the month) to rake in several hundred dollars from the gambling alone. Money was also made from selling food and drinks. Mamma Braxton and her helper(s), usually her faithful daughter-in-law Callie, who lived down the street, would begin to clean chitterlings, pick greens, and clean chickens first thing in the morning.

I got excited just thinking about the mouthwatering fried chicken that was to be served in only a few hours.

Up until this time, I maintained that I was a follower of the Muslim faith, although I followed hardly any of the religion's tenets. I used all kinds of drugs, had illicit sex, smoked cigarettes and anything else I had a mind to do. About the only Islamic practice I clung to was the prohibition against eating pork. For two years I did not eat pork. This practice did not sit well with Mamma Braxton. All of her life she felt extremely blessed to have any kind of meat to eat. She often ridiculed my refusal to eat the "flesh of the swine." She didn't care much for the fact that I professed to be a Muslim, but she never harassed me about it.

It was during one of these gambling parties that I finally denounced any ties to Islam. I sat playing cards at the dining room table, watching as my fellow partiers dined on snow white chitterlings dowsed in generous portions of Louisiana Hot Sauce with tasty sweet cole slaw on the side. I could stand it no more, not for one more minute. I had been raised eating chitterlings. I had loved eating them when Mamma prepared them at home on special occasions, such as Thanksgiving and Christmas. As I watched others enjoy this ghetto delicacy, I could resist no more. I must have some. I succumbed to the urge and ordered a plate of chitterlings.

"What did he say?" asked Lanard's sister-in-law, Willamae. "I know you didn't ask fa no chit'lins with yo Mooslim self, Joe."

"Yes I did," I replied. "I gotta have some of dem chit'lins. I guess I ain't no Muslim no more."

A roar of laughter went up from those seated around the dining room table and those seated and standing in the living room. Mamma Braxton must have thought that she would die of laughter when she heard those words. She watched with great delight as I gobbled the hog guts that she had prepared with her own hands. She was pleased that I had given up what she felt was a foolish notion, both being a Muslim and not eating pork.

"I knew dat boy couldn't stay here and see all dese good 'ole poak chops and chit'lins I be fixin' in here and keep talkin' 'bout he don't eat no poak. Look at dat boy eat dem chit'lins." The idea of my renouncing Islam for a plate of chitterlings was a joke that still circulates through the Braxton family. But now for the first time since I was nine years old, I was totally without a God, like a sheep without a shepherd. I had been disappointed with my experience as a Christian and disillusioned by my experience with Islam. For the next five years I would wander aimlessly in a spiritual waste-land. I did not believe that God was the god of the Christians, or the god of the Muslims, or even that He existed at all.

Alcohol was also for sale during these marathon gambling par-ties. Usually, several different types of whiskey and beer were avail-able to the consumer. The consumption of alcohol was a guarantee that something interesting would transpire before the night was over. Daddy Braxton was a known alcoholic. I can't remember a weekend, party or not, that he did not manage to acquire and con-sume enough whiskey and beer to make dealing with him a chal-lenge. He was the kind of alcoholic that was stimulated by drink-ing. He became very animated, constantly chattering and moving about. He stood about 5' 9" tall and was made of mostly gristle and wiry muscle. Even his short-cropped hair was wiry. He always wanted his share of the cut money off the top. Mamma Braxton always insisted that he wait until the party was over and the take was split equitably. This answer never satisfied him. He would stand waving his slender but powerful arms widely as he threatened to overturn the dining room table, thus ending the game, if he did not get his share of the money immediately.

It seemed that the only person who could calm Daddy Braxton down was his second youngest son, Damond. Just about everybody called Damond "Junior," although to this day I do not understand why. He was not the oldest, nor was he named after Daddy Braxton. He simply was called Junior. Like his dad, Junior was slender and wiry. He was a couple of inches taller than his father and about five shades darker. In fact, we speculated that Junior had a complex about his skin color. The fact that he stuttered, especially when excited, did not help his self-esteem any either. Yet something about his demeanor or his relationship with Daddy Braxton seemed to have a calming effect on him. Usually, Junior was able to keep the alcohol demon inside his father at bay at least until the game was over.

Actually, Daddy Braxton's style of drinking was part of a classi-cal pattern of drinking in the black community that dates back to slavery. He was what is called a weekend binger. For the most part, he managed to stay sober during the week. He was able to work his odd jobs and take care of whatever other business that might arise. However, it was a given that by Friday night Daddy Braxton would be intoxicated somewhere.

This is a pattern that holds with many black men, especially those of his generation and earlier. In the times of slavery, the slaves would work hard all day, engaged often in mindless menial labor. The masters would tolerate no less. During the week there was little if any time for rest and relaxation. Saturday evening, however, was designated as a time that they could "let their hair down," so to speak. Sunday was a day of rest and worship. But Saturday was a day to unwind and release the tension that was built up during the week. The master would supply the slaves with whiskey on Saturday night, not because they wanted to be nice to them, but because they knew that this was an effective way of controlling them, to keep them from thinking too much, from plotting. Obviously, this practice led to many fights and, no doubt, an occasional killing due to all the pent-up frustrations being released through alcohol consumption. To this day in the ghetto, Saturday night is still referred to as "niggers night," a phrase that was coined in slavery time. To this day, many blacks celebrate the end of the long, hard work week in the same manner as our slave fathers did.

I give the Braxtons credit for introducing me to hard liquor and the low-down dirty blues. These were the two constants of a Braxton weekend of partying. You could be sure to hear B.B. King, Bobby "Blue" Bland, Albert King, etc., and you could be certain that plenty of hard whiskey would be consumed. Prior to becoming a Williams-Braxton, my drinking was confined mostly to beer and wine. Lanard was the first youth our age, besides Martin, who regularly drank hard liquor. With him and a few other friends, I became acquainted with the hard stuff. While heroin and marijuana put me in a "mellow" mood, alcohol seemed to cause me to be more lively and jovial. Slowly, I grew to like drinking whiskey with the Braxtons and in other social settings. This was yet another tool in my bag of tricks. Actually, I was only tricking myself into thinking that I was dealing with my problems.

An alcohol high turned out to be multifaceted, however. Although it gave me a lift when I first drank it, after a while, if I sat too long, I became sleepy. Such was the case one night when Daddy Braxton was no longer satisfied to rant and rave and decided to get physical with his wife. Mamma Braxton had grown weary of listening to his carryings on and had decided she needed to tune him out in order to concentrate on the blackjack game. My money had run out a bit earlier. My body and mind slowly gave in to the relaxing effect of all the drinks I had downed. I passed out in my favorite chair beside the dining room wall. I slept soundly as the party moved into the wee hours of the morning.

From out of the dimly lit hallway that led from the kitchen and bedrooms, Daddy Braxton sprang with surprising quickness. "Frankie, I told you I want my money," he yelled, wielding a brown beer bottle in his bony hands. Before Mamma Braxton or anyone else could react, he crashed the bottle into the side of his unsuspecting wife's head.

Pandemonium immediately spread throughout the room. Mamma Braxton let out a loud groan and clutched her wounded head. Damond was able to subdue his father before he swung the bottle again. "What's wrong with you? Are you crazy? Hittin' Mamma like that. Mamma, you alright?" Damond questioned. Lanard assisted his stunned mother into her bedroom, which was located in the extreme rear of the four-family flat.

Junior was able to once again work his magic on his enraged father. Daddy Braxton sat, much calmer, but still fussing quietly to himself about why he had to wait until morning to get his money. After all, he had paid his share of the rent and lights. Then from out of the same dimly lit hallway emerged a furious Mamma Braxton pointing the family's .22 caliber rifle directly at her husband. She was tired of the abuse and did not intend to take it one second longer.

"I'm gon' kill you, nigger. You don' hit me fo' the last time," she announced with the end of the barrel trained at the frightened Daddy Braxton.

"Frankie, Frankie, no," he pleaded. His pleas were not sufficient, though, to curtail the wrath she intended to pour out on him for the long years of physical abuse he had doled out to her. Bang! The rifle exploded, leaving everyone in the room breathless.

Daddy Braxton was surprised to learn that there was no new hole in his tough old body. Either Mamma Braxton was a bad aim or she was merely aiming to scare some sense into the old man. The single shot evidently frightened her as much as it had frightened everyone else in the house. From that point she was content to sternly warn her mate not to ever think about hitting her again.

I had managed to sleep soundly through the entire experience, only learning of what had happened the next morning when I awoke. Lanard showed me that the bullet had lodged in the wall directly opposite where my head had rested. Apparently, a slat in the wall stood between my head and the bullet. Everyone marveled that I had managed to sleep through the whole experience. I marveled that I woke up.

Heroin had become a part of my drug experience when I hung out with Martin and Greg. Then, though, I did not like it nearly as much as I liked smoking weed. By now heroin was deeply entrenched in ghettos across this country. Lanard, other friends, and I began to deepen our love affair with this devastating drug that would scar all, dominate most, and destroy many who were foolish enough to flirt with it.

Lanard and the friends he hung out with were not what I considered criminals. They smoked weed, drank liquor, and snorted scag on a regular basis. This alone in the eyes of many was enough to classify them as criminals. They did not, however, commit crimes at that time to support their drug and alcohol usage.

Heroin had become so pervasive in the neighborhood that it seemed to me at the time that just about everyone under the age of thirty used it. Of course, this was not true. However, many of my peers used heroin at least on an occasional basis.

At this time Lanard and I used heroin on a recreational basis. We spent many weekend evenings engaged in snorting jive on his living room sofa after his parents were in bed. We were typically joined by several friends.

Charlie Wilson lived down the street from my parents on Otsego. Charlie was the shortest of the group. He was the product of a single-parent home. His parents had been divorced for a number of years. Charlie was not a good hustler, nor did he appear to be very fond of working. He was usually supplied his hang-out money by his mother, or on rare occasions by his father. Charlie loved acting silly, especially playing practical jokes.

Ron Fisher, a tall, dark brown-skinned, slender fellow, lived just around the corner from the Braxtons. Ron lived with his mother and stepfather in a small apartment. His mother believed in letting children have their way. Neither she nor Ron's natural father would hear of his stepfather disciplining him. As a result he was a pretty spoiled guy. Ron, too, was supplied most of his money by his parents.

Harry Tyler was tall, dark brown-skinned, and muscular. Harry, too, was the product of a single-parent home. His mother had left Louisiana with her three children in tow when Harry was about five years old. Eventually, she became involved with a fellow who made a living by selling drugs. He, too, became abusive to her. She shot him to death during one of those violent encounters. She became a heroine to us young guys because she had the nerve to take someone else's life. Harry's mother became even more of a heroine to us when we learned that she had become a major drug dealer herself. Ironically, she had no idea that while she peddled this poison to others, someone else was selling it to her own son. She was crushed when she found out a few years later that Harry had been using. Because of his mother's vocation, Harry usually had plenty of money to spend on himself and often others.

We would get together in the early evening to decide what we were going to do for entertainment on a weekend night. Increasingly, the decision was made to "cop some jive" (buy some heroin) and hang out at Lanard's house. All our money would go into one pot. Heroin was dirt cheap in those days. Our tolerance to the drug was not yet high, so we usually could purchase enough drugs to ensure that all of us would experience a "good" high.

The heroin came in either small red capsules or small packets of aluminum foil. It was dumped onto a record album cover. A thin, sturdy card, often a driver's license, was used to break up the caked-up white powder. Sometimes the powder was separated into short lines and snorted through a plastic straw. Other times we simply dipped into the pile with the card, snorting the drugs directly off the card.

When the drugs were particularly potent (one could never be sure how potent they were at the time of purchase), we became pathetic specimens, all of us. Voices began to drag and become gravelly. Mouths turned down on the sides. Eyelids drooped as the "nod" began to take effect. First, light scratching began by all (a result of the quinine that was used to cut the drug). Before the night was over, the itching would be so intolerable that zippers were unzipped as we rammed our hands down our pant legs in order to scratch our skin directly. Scratching through the fabric of the pants was no longer good enough.

Also, the drug caused its users to become quite irritable and, subsequently, argumentative. So all night as the stereo softly played Isaac Hayes, Eddie Kendricks, or some other beloved R&B artist, we scratched, we drooled, we nodded and argued as the album cover passed from one unsuspecting soul to the next. Sniff, sniff!

Living with the Braxtons was one of the pleasurable, albeit brief, moments of my young life. Mamma Braxton treated me with almost as much tenderness as she treated her biological children. Daddy Braxton also had a special regard for me, but for a practical reason. He clearly recalled a time when Martin, Greg, and I had observed him coming from the liquor store around the corner from his home. Martin wanted to beat him and mug him for whatever small change he may have had in his pocket. Because Lanard had been my friend for so long, I could not be a part of such an act. I successfully persuaded them to let him go unharmed. He never forgot.

I was not the only recipient of the Braxtons' benevolence down through the years. As I enjoyed my status as an adopted family member, another needy soul showed up in search of a respite. Mac was a close friend of Junior's. He had come to Detroit a few years earlier from Chicago. Mac was from one of Chicago's roughest neighborhoods. He freely bragged about the violence he had exacted on his many victims back in his hometown. Since he had been in Detroit, his violent lifestyle had continued. He had earned a reputation as being perfectly willing to engage in violent acts of all kinds. His parents were old family friends of the Braxtons. When he showed up at the Braxton house in need of shelter, Mamma Braxton could not turn him down.

"Mac stole my money and I know it," Mamma Braxton declared, following Junior into the dining room. "He's got to get outta here. I cain't have nobody living under my roof stealin' my money, Junior."

"How you know he the one who stole yo' money, Mamma?" Junior answered, acting as an advocate for Mac. "You can't prove he stole the money."

"Who else in here could'a stole my money. He ain't been here but a couple of weeks and money come up missin'. Ain't no money been missin'," she claimed. "Dat boy got to go."

"Joe coulda stole the money, Mamma," Junior replied. "He ain't no angel. His mouth ain't no prayer book."

My heart sank as I heard the words of accusation. *Surely*, I thought, *he could not be suggesting that I would bite the hand that was feeding me.* There was no way that this accusation could come to anything.

"You always takin' up for Lanard and his friends. You always take his side against mine. If you put Mac out, you gotta put Joe out too," Junior demanded.

I sat on the Braxtons' front porch enjoying the cooling late summer evening breeze. I dined on my usual staple of Lay's barbecue potato chips and Faygo red pop. It had been an hour or so since the heated exchange between Junior and his mother. I hoped that no news was good news. Mac had already been told that he had to leave. As far as I was concerned, it was good riddance. He got what he deserved. How dare he steal from Mamma Braxton after she had been so kind to us? Perhaps now this entire issue would blow over with no ill effects for me.

The expression on Lanard's yellowish tan face was not reassuring as he emerged from the downstairs flat after a long conversation with Mamma Braxton.

I could tell that the news would not be good.

"Mamma say you can't live here no more, Bro Joe, man," Lanard managed to choke out. "Junior is actin' a fool and he won't back down. Bro Joe, you know I love you and you will always be my brother. But Mamma say you got to go."

I had unwittingly become a pawn between the sibling rivalry of Lanard and his older brother. Mamma Braxton loved both of them. Junior, however, always felt that he was the least loved between him and his youngest brother. He was dark skinned; Lanard was light skinned. He stuttered while Lanard enjoyed the gift of gab. He had met with failure in school; Lanard was an excellent student.

Mamma Braxton felt she had to sacrifice me so that there could be peace between her boys, within her household. If expelling me from the family would bring about that peace, then it was a price worth paying. Mamma Braxton, as I could tell, was heartbroken at having to make such a decision.

How could this be happening to me? How could it be that I was losing yet another family? If only my life could be like that of the other boys I hung out with—like Lanard, Ron, Harry, or Charlie. If I could just live in the home of my own parents without fear of harm, in peace, entertaining dreams of one day becoming some- body. If only I did not have to be a sojourner at such a young age. But then, if only a bullfrog had wheels, he wouldn't bump his behind. He would just roll on.

5

ALL DOGS GO TO HEAVEN

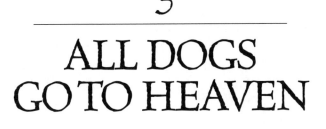

By the fall of 1971, the city had become increasingly more violent, and so had I. Street murders were becoming as commonplace as fried chicken at a family picnic. Heroin was the indisputable king of the ghetto, at least as far as my crowd and I were concerned. Violent turf wars erupted quickly, leaving in their wake hundreds of casualties every year. Detroit was soon to become known as the murder capital of the world. There was no doubt in my mind that soon I would become either a murder victim or a murderer. I would not be able to escape this inevitability for much longer.

Jesse James Wiley was Sister's oldest son. It was strange considering him as my nephew since he was ten years my elder. We got a kick out of people's reaction when they learned that I, a teenager, was actually his uncle.

Jesse James, as we sometimes called him, was an ex-offender who had a serious drinking problem. He had served three years in prison for being the getaway driver in an armed robbery. Prison had been a very difficult psychological adjustment for him. Once released, he was never the same Jesse.

Jesse was short, standing about 5' 8" tall. His skin was medium brown with a red tinge to it. Women, generally, found him to be attractive, at first. Once they learned of his uncontrollable personality and occasional episodes of violence, most soon shied away. It was because of this unpredictable and violent behavior that his wife, Eileen, had left him, along with their two sons.

While together, they purchased a small bungalow in the northwest section of Detroit. By this time, in 1971, the ghetto was expanding. After the 1967 riots there was a steady exodus of whites fleeing the city. They left behind beautiful brick homes located in attractive neighborhoods. All one needed was a steady job and a decent credit report to get into one of these abandoned jewels. Good-paying factory jobs were plentiful at that time. Consequently, in a brief period, many nice, white, middle-class neighborhoods changed into black, working-class, barbecue smoke–filled, soul music-emanating neighborhoods. Jesse's neighborhood was one of these. With Eileen now gone, Jesse's small house became a perfect place for me to hole up for a while. He extended the invitation for me to live there, renting one of the two bedrooms, and I gladly accepted.

Dedee and Rich had a rented house only two long blocks down from Jesse's house on the same street. This was an added attraction for me. It was great living with Jesse in an environment whose only rules were to contribute to the household economy in any way you could. I had broken the second promise I had made to Mamma several months earlier. After leaving the Braxton household, I had very little incentive to continue school. Without a doubt the knowledge that her once bright boy had short-circuited his education broke my mother's heart. I rationalized that she must be well used to it by this time, if indeed one can ever become used to heartbreak.

At the time I came to live with Jesse, he was on an extended medical leave from Ford Motor Company. There was nothing physically wrong with him that rendered him incapable of working. He managed to get a crooked doctor to document a fictitious ailment. This ailment entitled him to an extended paid vacation. Consequently, he had plenty of free time, income, and a desire to party. Jesse's house became a place where the drug users and boozers of the neighborhood could come and hang out.

Drug users and boozers, young and old, became acquainted with my nephew in quick fashion, often frequenting his little bungalow. Even a band of hippies found their way to the small house on Northlawn Street. They came down on occasion to trade drugs with us. Heroin was not available in the suburbs. This special brand of poison, it seemed, was reserved for the dark-skinned children of America. These young whites were able to access more potent marijuana than we could get in the inner city. They also brought with them a wide variety of psychedelic drugs such as angel dust. Often these cross-cultural exchanges lasted from late evening until early the next morning.

Marvin Franklin lived down and across the street from Jesse. Marvin was about a year my junior, although he looked several years older. He lived with both his parents. His dad had suffered a nervous breakdown a few years earlier. Because of this, Mr. Franklin was not able to provide Marvin with any structure or correction. Marvin's mother was left to raise her strong-willed, oversized youngster the best she could. The Franklins had one other child, a girl, Ricki, who was about four years younger than Marvin.

The distance separating me from my own beloved neighborhood made it difficult to have much contact with Lanard, Charlie, Harry, and Ron. Marvin became a fast and convenient friend. Like me, he was an aspiring but still small-time criminal. Most importantly, we shared the same great love for heroin.

By this time, I had reached six feet in height. I was as skinny as a pencil due to not having a healthy diet. Marvin was about my height, but much broader and stronger. It was apparent that he had not missed many meals, while I had. Although only seventeen years old, we became friends, Marvin possessed a manly, sometimes menacing demeanor. I liked Marvin a lot because he was usually game for anything that involved girls, drugs, or making fast money.

Somehow, I had gotten hold of a raggedy old Saturday Night Special (.22 caliber pistol). It was not nearly as easy to buy a gun in those days in the underground market, especially for guys my age, as it is today. The unwritten code of the streets stipulated that older criminals did not provide their younger, more immature protégés with guns. It was considered bad business. No one back then wanted the kind of heat kids with guns would surely bring about.

It was Friday night in the fall of the year. Marvin had come over to hang out with me about an hour earlier. Jesse was out of the house. Although there were parties and cabarets going on all over town, we two did not have a dollar between us to take advantage of any of them. We could not have participated in the celebration of the coming of the weekend if we wanted to. If we had money we would not have used it to go to a party. We would have copped a blow (purchased some heroin).

"Where can we get some money from, man?" I quizzed a bored-looking Marvin. "I'm tired of sittin 'round the crib (house) lookin' stupid. I want to get cool (high)."

"As soon as the sun goes down we can break into the gas station. That's always good for fifty dollars," Marvin suggested.

"Naw, we done played that out. They gotta get hip to us breakin' in there all the time. We gotta try something different," I countered.

Marvin had been employed at the corner gas station for several years. His employment had ended about a year earlier. He knew where the owner kept fifty dollars in small bills in the station. We used that knowledge as a standby. If we couldn't get money from anyplace else, we could break into the corner gas station. Surprisingly, they kept putting the fifty dollars in the same place. We kept stealing it.

"I got a idea," I offered. "Why don't we call the pizza man and rob him when he comes," I continued, as I turned the bullets in the chamber of my pistol.

"He might not have enough money to make it worthwhile," Marvin complained. "I don't wanna rob nobody and don't even get enough money to get high with."

"This is what we can do," I suggested. "We'll call and order a pizza, tell them to bring two packs of Kools (cigarettes) and a large Coke. We can tell them that we have a fifty-dollar bill, so the driver has to bring enough change."

"That sounds cool," Marvin answered enthusiastically. "Yeah, that's cool, let's do it."

I placed the phone call to the local pizza joint, ordering the biggest pizza with as many toppings as I could think of. The person who took the order agreed to make certain the driver had change for $50. We gave the address to the house next door. We knew that no one was at home. After about a half an hour Marvin and I went outside to wait for the unsuspecting driver. The pistol in my hand gave me a sense of power that I had never known before. Several of my friends had embarked on careers of armed robbery. Often we sat around bragging about our adventures. One young man I grew up with had already shot several of his robbery victims. He shared every terrible detail about one instance when he held a sawed-off shotgun to the head of his victim and ordered him not to move. The man either moved involuntarily or flinched. In any event, the result was the same. He shot him in the head, killing him.

In these informal crime symposiums, we instructed each other on the finer points of particular crimes. I learned never to stand for the disobedience of a victim during a robbery. One would lose control of the situation if he allowed an order to go unheeded. I listened intently to the principles shared during these times of instruction. These sessions stimulated me to no end. I eventually became addicted to sticking up. I anxiously awaited an opportunity to pop (shoot) someone so I could go back and prove to the others that I was as much of a wolf as they all were.

Finally, the delivery man's car pulled in front of the house. Psychedelic rock music blared from the car's stereo system. My heart beat so wildly and loudly that I feared he would be able to hear it. Adrenaline soared to every inch of my body. The rusty .22 caliber pistol felt like a cannon in my slim hand. I had the power.

We crouched, coiled, like ravenous animals ready to pounce upon a hapless prey, on the side of the house. Watching intently as the hippie-type deliveryman bounded from the car, pizza, pop, and Kools in hand, we waited until he reached the short concrete porch, then sprang into action.

"Git yo' hippie   aroun' here," I uttered in the most sinister voice I could manage. My intention was to thoroughly intimidate him from the start by the use of my voice, facial expression, demeanor, and gestures. This would keep him on his heels and me in control, I believed.

The driver froze in his tracks, seeing us two desperate-looking black youths. "OK man, everything is cool," he attempted to assure us. "You can have all this   . I don't care about this   ."

He walked slowly from the porch to where we crouched, beckoning him to an uncertain fate on the side of the house. Marvin firmly grabbed his arms and shoved him in the direction of the alley. The smell of marijuana reeked from the driver's clothes. The knowledge that he was probably high was disturbing to me. It meant that he might react in an unpredictable manner. Not that I would have minded shooting him. But if it came to that, I wanted to pick my spot.

It soon became obvious that he was intoxicated. Had he been sober he might have been more appreciative of the danger he faced. He moved much more slowly than I would have liked to see him move, almost floating as we coaxed him toward the backyard. In frustration I gave him a hard shove in the back.

"You betta git yo' hippie   to movin' before I bust a cap in yo'   ," I threatened.

My anger began to rise quickly, my face becoming hot and itchy, as he continued to mope along. "Be cool, man. I'm not gonna give you no trouble," he attempted to assure me.

His continued lack of response soon drove my emotions from anger to fury. My eyes began to squint as my breathing became more labored. He didn't know it, but by being so unresponsive he was challenging my personhood. I wanted him to know that I was a force to be reckoned with. I was important, had power; his very life was in my hands. It appeared to be no more than a joke to him. He was fronting me off and I did not like it one bit. I had to do something to save face, I thought.

Finally, we reached the alley where Marvin relieved him of the pizza, pop, and cigarettes. I stuck my hand into his pocket, retrieving the wad of bills he carried. We had what we wanted.

"Now run!" I ordered him as I planted my foot squarely in his behind. Again, he was unresponsive to my command. Perhaps, because of the influence of the drugs he was under, he was not able to move any faster. All I knew was that he was not giving me my props (proper respect), me, the man with the gun. I had no choice but to shoot him in order to teach him a lesson and to save face with Marvin.

My heart was pounding rapidly and hard as I raised my arm parallel with my shoulder, pointing the end of the barrel at the back of his head. He continued to take his sweet time loping down the alley. Marvin stood rigid beside me. I aimed, feeling the stiff trigger against the flesh of my bony finger. My chest heaved as I applied pressure to the trigger. Then a final squeeze. But instead of the loud pop I expected to hear, a sickly sounding click, barely loud enough to hear two feet away, came from the undependable source of power I wielded. Frustrated that the gun had not fired, I pulled the trigger again. "Click," the gun responded.

"Nigga, you crazy!" Marvin protested. "You got the money; let's get the   out of here," he demanded.

Dropping my hand with the pistol clutched in it to my side, I turned quickly and followed Marvin into the yard. That night we feasted on pizza and Coke, snorted dope, and smoked cigarettes to our hearts' content. The next night Marvin and I went back into the alley to test the gun. I pointed the pistol into the air and squeezed the trigger. Pop! went the pistol, spitting a small spray of fire into the dark night. Again I squeezed the trigger. Again the gun exploded, propelling another slender shaft of lead into the air. Marvin and I stood there for a moment staring at each other in amazement.

That night God spared the life of the pizza driver. Also, He spared me from becoming a cold-blooded murderer.

Dedee and Rich hadn't been getting along well for a couple of years. Rich was no longer employed at the auto factory. Now, he made his living totally in the fast life. He had sunk deeper and deeper into heroin addiction as well.

Dedee had grown tired of the up-and-down lifestyles the streets often afforded. She was tired of juggling bills and not having enough money for her and her now three-year-old son she and Rich called Wee (or Wee Wee), because he was such a small baby when he was born. Finally, she decided it was time to part company with Rich.

Rich had informed her that he would not allow her to leave with anything he had bought for her. If she chose to leave, she must only take what she had on her back. He should have realized that attempting to bully a woman who grew up with five brothers would not likely work. Dedee called me at Jesse's house to ask for safe escort while she packed and hauled away her meager possessions. I didn't have to think twice about whether to help my sis.

By now I had given up my unreliable popgun for a man's weapon. I purchased a twelve-gauge pump shotgun and had the barrel sawed off. This sawed-off pump became dearly beloved to me. I cleaned it, polished it, unloaded and loaded it constantly. I was absolutely enamored with its potential power.

When Dedee called, I promptly doned my full-length black cashmere coat. Picking up the shotgun from the corner where it rested and concealing it under my coat gave me a feeling of being dressed for success. The relationship between Rich and me had deteriorated greatly by now. Even if it hadn't, though, I would have fought him up and down the alley all night and all day long to protect my sister.

When I got to Dedee's house, she and Wee Wee were there alone. Dedee was gathering her belongings, placing them into a large black plastic garbage bag. I stood guard at the door while she finished her hasty packing. If Rich came while we were there and started something, I was prepared to blow him away.

Rich never showed up—thank God. Dedee and I started down the street toward Jesse's house, lugging the heavy garbage bag and Wee Wee. It was very awkward for me trying to carry the over-stuffed bag while holding and concealing the shotgun under my coat.

We had nearly reached the halfway mark of our journey when a familiar enemy made his presence known to us. We froze in our tracks as we heard the steady growl of the large brown boxer coming from the nearby porch of a house on the same side of the street we were on. The vicious dog had often chased us on our way to and from Jesse's house. I had experienced a couple of narrow escapes by jumping on top of parked cars. But how could we escape his attack this time, having the large bag to carry and Wee Wee at our side?

"Don't run," I ordered Dedee, dropping the plastic bag to the concrete sidewalk. "If he comes off that porch I'm gon' blow him away."

Dedee froze beside me, clutching her frightened preschooler close to her leg. The boxer sprang from the porch heading for me and my charges. Casually, I raised the shotgun and pointed it directly at the rushing dog. I waited until he was about five feet in front of me and squeezed the hard trigger.

Fire sprayed from the short barrel of the shotgun. Some of the buckshot struck the pavement of the sidewalk, creating a firework-like effect from the sparks. Terror flashed into the eyes of the dog as the force of the blast sent him back about six feet. He let out a deafening yelp of pain and horror. Severely injured, he continued back toward the porch from which he had charged, performing a hideous dance as he went.

Suddenly, the front door of the house swung open. Two young men rushed out of the house screaming, "You shot my dog! You shot my dog! I'll kill you!" They attempted to offer comfort to their wounded friend while assuring me of their displeasure of my terrible act.

Quickly, I glanced at Dedee. "Now it's time to run," I suggested to her.

Dedee picked up Wee Wee and took off running toward Jesse's house as fast as her slender bowlegs would carry her. I grabbed the bag from the pavement and ran down the street with the shotgun in my hand in plain sight. We could hear all kinds of commotion behind us. "Just keep running," I yelled to Dedee, who quickly began to tire.

In order to get back to the safety of Jesse's house, we had to cross a busy street. We must have been a sight crossing that street carrying the large garbage bag, baby, and shotgun. We made it to the other side. It felt like we had conquered a great barrier. I pushed Dedee towards the mouth of the alley, which led to the back door of Jesse's house. This was the same alley I had almost shot the pizza delivery man in only months earlier. We were almost at the alley when our pursuers overtook us.

"Screeeeech," went the awful sound of tire rubber burning against the asphalt as the Thunderbird swerved to a halt in an attempt to cut us off. *Well, it's come to a shoot-out,* I thought to myself. I was convinced that it was better to kill than to be killed. My gut drew taut as the two men sprang from the car and rushed towards my family members and me. There was no doubt in my mind that they had come well armed and ready to engage in urban battle. The warrior inside of me refused to back down.

As both men ran toward me, I pushed Dedee and her child onto the ground beside a nearby fence and out of the line of expected fire. Once again the short barrel of the shotgun was raised away from the cold ground and aimed in the direction of a living creature. My finger began applying pressure to the cool trigger as I pumped another shell into the chamber.

Seeing the barrel of the shotgun pointed at him, the man in the lead tried to put on brakes. He fell backwards as his feet slipped out from under him. "Don't shoot! Please don't kill me," he pleaded as he crawled backwards, resembling a huge crab.

Imagine the scene: one tall, skinny kid, standing on the sidewalk of a busy city street holding a sawed-off shotgun. Nearby, a woman and a small child lay motionless on the ground. Finally, an automobile turned sideways, partially blocking the street, its former occupants now scrambling for their lives in a mad attempt to flee the expected blast from the powerful weapon. People passing by in their cars must have thought they were hallucinating. It was amazing to me that they pursued us without even a penknife. Relief soon washed over me as I realized that I may not have to shoot anyone over something so stupid. Why didn't they simply keep their dog in the house?

We were not out of the woods yet, though. We still had to make it the rest of the way home. Dedee lay over on the ground panting in exhaustion. "I can't make it, Bro Joe, I'm too tired," she gasped.

It never dawned on her to leave the bag and simply escape with her life. "Look," I told her, "I'm gonna take Wee Wee to Jesse's, go down the alley, and be back for you."

Scooping up the boy under my arm and carrying the gun in my free hand, I made my way down the street towards Jesse's, staying close to the well-trimmed hedges in front of the houses. Finally, I made it. Bursting through the front door of Jesse's house, I tossed Wee Wee onto the couch.

"They've got Dedee. I gotta go back and find her," I blurted to a stunned Jesse.

"What's the matter?" Jesse demanded.

"I shot that dog down up the street. They chased us. I gotta go back for Dedee." I huffed and puffed as I ran to the back door.

Stopping in Jesse's backyard, I listened to determine if I could hear Dedee or her pursuers, or both. Cautiously, I moved to the alley softly calling for Dedee. A figure darted from behind a garbage can about ten feet to my left side. Swinging my shotgun around, I was relieved to find that it was Dedee.

"Don't shoot," she panted, holding her arm straight out in front of her as if her hand could have stopped a spray of buckshot. "Don't shoot, Bro Joe—it's me."

Grabbing my exhausted sister under her armpit, I dragged her into the house. It was astounding to me that we had been able to make it safely to Jesse's. We plopped down into chairs as we caught our breath and gathered our wits.

After regaining my composure to a small degree, I decided to call for reinforcements in the event we were spotted at any time entering the house. Perhaps they were planning to attack us yet, I reasoned.

"Marvin, can you come over right away and bring your piece, man? Don't ask no questions. Just come on now," I pleaded with my friend, barely giving him enough time to get the receiver to his ear.

Within five minutes there was a knock on the door. Marvin walked through the door waving his arms wildly in the air. "Man, I was just comin' down the street and some niggas grabbed me and stuck a pistol in my face. I thought I was dead. Then the other one said, 'That ain't him,' and they let me go. They kept sayin' something about somebody shot their dog."

Then Marvin turned to me in an accusatory tone. "You shot dat dog didn't you?"

"Yeah, I shot him. Almost shot his masters, too. Fool come runnin' up on me like he had something. I pumped one in the chamber and was getting ready to blast him. You should have seen him put on brakes and get the   outta there. They ought to keep that mutt in the house," I retorted.

Dedee and I spent the next half an hour giving the details of our ordeal to Jesse and Marvin. Everyone was amazed that the episode had ended with only a dog getting shot. We all knew that it could have been much worse.

I didn't recognize back then how miraculously God was protecting me from others as well as myself. Then I attributed it to luck or skill. Now, of course, looking back I realize that God had His angels protecting me until I was ready to return to the sheepfold.

But for now, Dedee was without a home, without a man to protect her. We had to put our heads together to come up with a plan for survival. Jesse James certainly could not house all of us for long. As we contemplated our uncertain future, I could hear Wee Wee explaining to Jesse what happened that night. "Uncle Joe shot the doggie, boom!"

6

NIGHT OF
THE NARCS!

By the time I was nineteen years old, I was a veteran drug dealer. Dedee and I lived together in a small two-bedroom frame house on the northwest side. Our arrangement was that she would take care of some household expenses with her welfare check. I would take care of the rent and some other household expenses from my drug dealing income. This arrangement seemed to be working quite well for a time.

It had been nearly four years since I had left my parents' home on Otsego. Yet it seemed that it had been decades since I left. Although I still frequented the neighborhood to visit my buddies and Mamma, I had nearly lost all parochial ties to it. I had gained the confidence to venture out into different areas of the city as well as different criminal ventures. No one who knew me during this phase of my life would have ever believed that I had evolved from the sweet-faced, fifteen-year-old junior usher at Greater New Mt. Moriah Missionary Baptist Church—a lamb.

Actually, my own heart had grown so much colder, my thinking so different that I barely recognized myself. I had traveled a long way from home, although I still only lived about four miles from my childhood neighborhood. Now, I carried a handgun almost all of the time. This was stock-in-trade for the urban drug dealer. It was like the American Express Card. I never left home without it. I was never the kind to start a conflict. I did not believe I would hesitate to shoot someone to protect my family, my business interests, or myself. I guess everyone else believed it as well, so I never was called upon to prove it.

I stayed as far away from the church as possible. I even began to ridicule Mamma and others for being a part of an institution that performed no tangible service to anyone. As far as I could tell, the people simply went there, listened to the choir (admittedly the choirs truly could sing), listened to the preacher, and at some point in the service, everyone threw a bunch of hard-earned money in the collection plate in order to support the preacher's lifestyle. The black urban church certainly had its critics in that era. For the first time in history, the black church, which had for years been the backbone of the black community, really struggled in an attempt to prove her relevance in society. In the 60s black militant leaders had risen trumpeting popular phrases such as "black power," "by any means necessary," "burn baby, burn," in essence usurping the elders of the black community, the pastors. The young black leaders managed to draw a great number of young men out of the church and into the streets. The pastors failed to adequately respond to this challenge to their leadership. This resulted in the church losing perhaps an entire generation of black men.

The black church had not foreseen the great changes that occurred in the 60s. Now in the 70s she appeared to be light years behind the times socially. It would be another decade before she would begin to regain her place of significance in the community. Our church had not addressed our family's issues of domestic violence and verbal abuse. It had not saved Mamma from her personal hell; nor was it able to rescue me from my tormentor. It seemed to have no answer for the drug epidemic. As far as I was concerned, I would never return to the church to fork over my hard-earned dough to some pimp in a black dress. Of course, this perception of the church was incorrect. However, the way that one perceives a thing is often more powerful than the truth.

Speaking of pimps, for a hundred years after slavery they had been the kings of all the black street hustlers. Other criminals admired the fact that these unschooled psychologists were able to so totally manipulate the lives of others. They had the mysterious ability to absolutely rule over some of the most beautiful women in the community—women so attractive that other men in the community and many from outside the community readily laid down good money in order to share a brief sexual encounter with them. These women entered into unwritten agreements with men from this special brand of wolves to sell their bodies either on a street corner or in a bordello, turning over all of their money to their pimps.

Pimps were usually the most financially successful, best-dressed, most attractively groomed men in criminal culture. They had the best, most glamorous cars, usually Cadillacs. They even drove differently than others. Pimps perfected an urban style of driving called "leaning." Leaning meant that the person driving, instead of driving in the upright position with both hands on the steering wheel like most, would lean his body over to the right, resting his arm on his armrest. While slowly cruising through the area most known for prostitution and other types of vice, the pimp would drive slowly, leaning with only his left hand, which was always jewelry clad, gripping the steering wheel. I imagine this body position was more conducive for them while checking their traps (periodically checking to see how much money their women had made and collecting it). Pimps were heard to recite lines of ghetto street poetry that related to their exalted status. This poetry almost always ridiculed those who worked for a living and women who did not sell their wares. One pimp proclaimed, "I don't do nothin' but lean and burn gasoline. All I do all day is pimp whoes (whores), drop Secoes (take a barbiturate sold on the streets), and slam Eldorado doaz (doors)."

The advent of heroin had created a different order in the ghetto criminal culture. Pimps fell on hard times as the economy in the streets shifted from traditional types of vice to drugs. Heroin, with its conquering army, came into the community taking no prisoners. The dopeman now replaced the pimp as king of the hustlers. Now it was the dopeman who drove the best cars, wore the finest clothes and jewelry, and had the finest women. And I was now a dopeman. My occupation provided me with a high status among my peers. Like Boo's place four years earlier, my place was becoming the hangout for up-and-coming street gangsters and hustlers, minus the French poodles. I was making money!

Marvin and I had decided to become partners in the drug trade. We pooled our money, bought a relatively small quantity of heroin, and began to deal. It wasn't long before word got out that we had a good quality product. Each time we sold a batch of heroin, we used the money to purchase larger quantities of drugs until we were able to purchase about a two-day supply. Eventually, we were making several hundred dollars per day, which in that day and time was a lot of money, especially for a nineteen-year-old. I had finally achieved my dream of becoming the "man." My wardrobe was quickly increasing. We were able to furnish the house with every kind of modern appliance. You see, once a person began to use heroin, it was not long before they would begin to sell all they had in order to acquire the drug. Marvin and I were happy to trade them drugs for jewelry, clothing, guns, and appliances. Some of the items we kept for ourselves. Others we sold at a nice profit. No one could touch me now that I had a pistol in my waistband, a bankroll in my pocket, and a sack of drugs on my coffee table (so I thought).

Mamma and Dad had another of their famous one-way fights. He hit her, and she hit the floor. Flesh marred, heart wounded, and ego bruised, Mamma decided to leave Dad and move in with Dedee and me. As incredible as it sounds, we decided to conduct business as usual, Mamma and all. I was convinced that I needed to sell drugs more than ever for the sake of the family's survival. We would use the money I made from drug dealing to get another place where we could all live. We would keep the current place for business purposes only. In the meantime, we would have to make do. Mamma didn't like the idea of my dealing drugs. Marvin, Deedee, and I assured her that we only sold a little harmless marijuana. We actually dealt almost exclusively in heroin. Her spirit severely wounded, Mamma retired to the bottle, and for most of the time she lived with us, she remained in an alcoholic fog.

My house was like Grand Central Station. People came and went at all hours of the day and night. The money was rolling in. I always had plenty of company. Everyone laughed at my jokes. We sold drugs from that house as if we had a license. We never got any heat from the police. That was true until we acquired some white customers from the suburbs. I didn't realize it then, but one of the unwritten laws of the ghetto stated that it was fine to sell heroin to other blacks. The person who dared to sell drugs to whites, though, usually had short careers in the drug business.

"What happened to the lights?" Dedee asked. "I thought you paid the light bill." "I did pay it," I responded. "There must be some kind of mistake by the electric company. A phone call should straighten this out." After calling the electric company we were assured the situation would be taken care of in the morning. Great! We had to spend the evening with no electricity.

March had brought with it a welcome relief from the harsh winter of 1971–72. Days were longer. Nights were warmer. As the sun began to drop behind our urban landscape, my partner Marvin and I began to dig in for what promised to be an interesting evening of conducting business by candlelight. A couple of my buddies from the old neighborhood were also with us in the house. Ron and Harry liked to hang out at my place. They would either come by to purchase drugs, beg for drugs from my other customers, or run errands for when I needed them. I liked having them around. I was confident that since we had all grown up together, should anything go down they would have my back. Mamma in no way approved of the business we were in, but she had made us swear that we would take care of one another no matter what.

Crash! Bam! Boom! Shlang-a-lang! It seemed that every window in the house was forcefully shattered at once. I had never heard such a commotion in my entire life. It was as if a war had begun right in my own home. "What the   ," I exclaimed to Marvin. We looked at each other in the dim light in terror and confusion. Only a month earlier four people had been found dead in a dopehouse on Hazelwood Street on the West Side of Detroit. They had also been robbed. Those responsible had not been caught yet. Could this be the same people from the Hazelwood massacre? I held the sawed-off pump shotgun tightly in my hands, determined to go down with a good fight should this be a drug stick-up.

Boom, boom! Someone was attempting to break down the front and back door. Finally, "Police," the officers shouted as they continued their assault. Quickly, I ran to the basement steps. Since this was the police and not the stick-up man, I knew better than to be caught with a shotgun in my hand. Also, having a sawed-off shotgun was a federal offense. Clang-a-lang! I tossed the sawed-off down the basement steps and dropped to the floor. "Don't move!" commanded the seemingly huge narc.

The Detroit Police narcotics squad was known for being particularly vicious and brutal. But then so were the drug dealers. I feared for my life as I lay helplessly on the floor with narcotics officers now swarming all over the house. Marvin was also face down on the floor only a few feet away. Harry and Ron were in the bedroom where I conducted business, I imagined in the same vulnerable position. More than my own safety and that of my associates, I feared for Mamma. What was happening to her? Before the raid, she had been lying in Dedee's bed in the back bedroom of this two-bedroom, one-story house. She had been drinking fairly heavily all evening. Because of that fact, I feared that she might react in a way that might bring harm to her.

From my position on the floor, I could hear the officers in the bedroom talking to Mamma. Her only concern was for the safety of my crew and me. She kept asking over and over, "Is my boy alright? What have you done with all my boys?" The officers were very kind to Mamma. That was quite a relief to me as I lay facedown on the thin carpet guarded by an officer who had the largest feet I had ever seen on a white man. They assured her that everyone was all right and that the situation was under control. I also heard them question her regarding whether she had any place to go since our home/drug den was now not fit to stay the night in.

My attention was diverted from Mamma when I heard an officer call from the basement. "Hey John, you should see what I found down here," he exclaimed. From the corner of my eye I could see him come through the door holding the sawed-off shotgun in his hand. "Look at what they had for us," he nearly shouted to his partner. It appeared that their adrenaline was pumping about as hard as ours was.

"Whose gun is this?" the officer questioned me. "It must be yours," I glibly replied. "You're the one holding it." Perturbed by my impertinent response, the officer stood over my head drawing back the shotgun with the butt facing my head. "I'm going to ask you one more time. Whose gun is this?" he demanded. "Get smart with me again and I'm going to crush your   head, boy," he assured me.

"Alright, alright, it's mine, it's mine," I acknowledged. "The shotgun is mine and anything else you want to be mine is mine, OK?" I cowered. My newly humbled attitude seemed to appease him as he slowly lowered the gun without striking me with it. He did utter a number of choice words expressing his displeasure with my character and lack of courage in the face of danger, before ordering the uniformed officers who had just arrived to haul me in to the station. As they ushered me out the door, handcuffed behind my back, I could hear Mamma once again pleading with them not to hurt me. Likewise, I prayed that she would be able to make it to some safe haven, although I did not have a clue as to what she would do now.

This was my first serious charge as an adult, although I had been to jail on several occasions for relatively minor offenses. Though I never saw my mug shot, I imagine I looked just like any other street tough one might view on *Cops* or *America's Most Wanted,* a common, small-time criminal. Looking at me, I am sure that most would dismiss me as any other menace to society, a slimy thug. Yes, I certainly was like many other criminals, more than I even knew at that time. You see, I almost perfectly fit the profile of most men in prison then and today. For two-thirds of prisoners come from broken homes. Ninety-five percent of the men in prison had no loving father figure as a role model. Two-thirds of those in prison are substance abusers. Fifty-percent of the men in prison have been physically or sexually abused. Forty-five percent of male prisoners were unemployed at their time of arrest. The overwhelming majority of prisoners cannot read or write well enough to get along well in society.

I was taken to the First Precinct police station, affectionately called the Gray Palace, to await a bail hearing. Bam had learned through Dedee that our house had been raided and that my associates and I were taken to jail. He knew of a lawyer who handled a lot of drug cases. While in the holding cell in the courthouse, Attorney Herman Padusko paid me a visit. Herman told me what his fee would be and assured me that because this was my first adult offense, I would be released on my own recognizance. My fellow cellmates and I awaited our turns to go before the judge. Of course, many war stories were exchanged during this time of fellowship. Some men were escorted before the bench, coming back into the holding cell minutes later, despondent at having been remanded to the Wayne County Jail. Hopefully, Herman was correct in his promise to me. Hopefully, prayerfully, I would not have the pleasure of being a guest of the County, nor later the guest of the State, for that matter.

It was a relief to look out into the courtroom and see my big brother, Bam. He gave me one of those I-got-your-back looks, and I began to feel better even before I stood before the bench. Herman was right. When I went before the judge, he released me on my own recognizance. Bam drove me back to the house. On the way he filled me in on all that had transpired during the brief time I had been in custody. Marvin and the others had been released earlier in the day. They had only been charged with loitering in a place of illegal occupation, while I was charged with violation of the state narcotic law. Mamma was alright. She had decided to go back home to Dad. I guess the excitement of living in a dope-house was a bit more than the old girl could stand. What a rotten failure I felt like. Finally, having the chance to do something for my poor, abused mother, I had miserably blown it, placing her in greater danger than she had ever faced at home with Dad on his worst day. What a shameful excuse for a son I had turned out to be! This incident would forever remain a monument to my youthful stupidity.

Seeing the house in the daytime allowed me to see what a war zone it truly looked like. Every window in the house was broken out. The front and back doors were both caved in. We had to work for hours just to secure the doors and windows so the place could be made livable. Naturally, the lights were back on. It seemed that Detroit Edison had conspired with the police department to have my lights turned off so they could come in under the advantage of darkness. It worked to perfection.

Marvin informed me that he was successful in flushing all the drugs down the toilet before the police got into the house. As it turned out, though, the police had brought their own drugs to plant in the event we were successful in getting rid of our stash. My charges stated that I had been caught with a small quantity of heroin. Because the police caused me to dispose of my drug products and seized my entire bankroll, my continued future as a drug dealer now looked bleak. I was afraid to try to sell drugs from that house again since the police now knew where we were located. Dedee and I sat in the small dining room contemplating our future now that my drug operation had been so rudely shut down.

The date was set for me to appear in court to stand trial. Herman had instructed me to be certain to have a job when I went to court. The judge, he said, would look more favorably upon me if I were working. The only job I managed to acquire was washing dishes at a private dinner club downtown called the Detroit Club. Lanard worked there as a busboy in training to be a waiter. He got me the job. I lost the job after only about a couple of months for missing too many days. My court date was drawing ever nearer. The judge had sent me threatening messages via my associates who had gone before him and received slaps on the wrists. According to Marvin, he was saving the real time for me.

Herman had a reputation of being a shrewd and capable lawyer. He was known for being able to keep his clients out of prison by hook or crook, mostly crook. He had assured me he could keep me out of prison for a fee. He was also known for making certain that those who tried to cross him by not paying his fee were convicted and sent to prison. This sent an unmistakable message to the other criminals not to try to mess with him. With no job and no hustle, my future began to look more and more as if Ionia Prison might be my home for a while. Ionia was the prison to which young adult offenders were sent. It was nicknamed "gladiator school" because it had such a reputation for violence. In gladiator school a guy would surely be tested to prove his worthiness of continuing in the game (criminal culture). I had heard tale after tale of many a young man being punked out in Ionia.

By this time I was 6'1" tall, weighing about 150 pounds, soaking wet. I was too light to fight and too thin to win, as the saying went. So, as you might imagine, I was not looking forward to spending the next few years defending my life and my manhood. However, with no money to pay Herman's fee and the judge breathing out threats, it had begun to look more and more as if Ionia was my destiny. I was petrified. I should have heeded the conventional street wisdom that warned, "Don't do the crime if you can't do the time."

Depression nearly totally overtook me during those days leading up to my trial. Nearly all of my so-called friends totally abandoned me. Once, my house was the place where everybody hung out, the place to be. Everything was happening there. I was funny, handsome, and cool. Now, though, that my drug operation was shut down and I didn't have any money, I was regarded pretty much as a slug. A hard lesson in human nature!

While awaiting trial, I received an interesting invitation in the mail from my uncle. This invitation informed me that today's modern army wanted me to be all that I could be. At first, I totally dismissed this draft notice, knowing that the army would not accept a person who had a criminal court case pending. Then it seemed as if a light came on over my bushy Afro. What if the army did not know of my criminal charges and pending prosecution? What if I simply reported as ordered for military duty like everyone who had been drafted in this lottery? The army might not be such a bad way to go. It was not unheard of for a judge to take a person's sterling military career into consideration. I could go into the army, do well, and then turn myself in after my tour. Surely the judge would see that I had successfully rehabilitated myself and decide there was no need to send me to prison. This could be the break I needed. I could go into the army, get away from the streets of Detroit, get away from the drug culture in which I was so thoroughly entangled, and finally make something decent of myself. At the time my brother Harold was in the army. He had been drafted about five years earlier. He seemed to truly like the military. We thought at that time he would make a career of it.

That was my plan. I would go into the army to get myself together. I would come back home in a couple of years and face my problems at that time. I had no way of knowing at that time how flawed that plan was. However, it was a straw. I was a drowning man. I had to grab on to it.

7

GI
JUNKIE

Springtime in Southwestern Germany may even rival springtime in my own home state of Michigan. Surprisingly, the weather was quite similar. The air was sweet and cool. Vegetation and foliage was lush and green. As I sat on the steps of my new barracks, I could only imagine what life for me would be like for the next thirteen months, my remaining time in Germany, and most likely the military. Getting into the army was every bit as easy as I had hoped. Apparently no one checked my criminal record.

The first part of the plan to redeem myself had gone extremely well. I had so far successfully avoided prosecution and imprisonment. My new environment, however, was not powerful enough to help me make the change I needed most, the change on the inside. On the contrary, upon entering the army I found that there were many young men just like myself. These young urban criminals had been charged with a crime serious enough for them to be sent to prison. The judge gave them the opportunity to enter into the army in order to avoid imprisonment. Should they successfully complete their term of service, the judge would then drop all pending criminal charges against them.

On the surface this act of charity on the part of the courts and the military might appear quite generous. One has to realize, though, that at this time the Vietnam War was still raging. In return for having their slates wiped clean, these young men were in turn agreeing to serve as cannon fodder in a war in which few people wanted to fight. The army of the 1970s was quite different from the army of today. Nowadays you have to be college material in order to be accepted. Back then, hardly anyone with two legs was turned down for service. High school dropouts, illiterates—all were welcome. The sole qualifying criteria appeared to be whether or not you could hold a gun.

These young men, though, were no more afraid of Vietnam than I was. Actually, when asked for my choices of assignments, I volunteered for Vietnam. Now, there was not a patriotic bone in my body. Nor had I gone totally insane. To me this decision made perfect sense. First of all, the best heroin in the world, China White, was grown and processed in that part of the world. I wanted to experience Ms. White in her pure form before I left this planet. If I had to go to Vietnam to do it, no problem! Knocking off a few of Uncle Sam's enemies in the process—well, that was cool too.

Second, the violence of Vietnam did not frighten my fellows and me as it may have frightened most. We were used to a very violent environment. I carried a gun before I went into the army more often than I did after I went in. Frankly, I lost immeasurably more friends and acquaintances to street violence than I ever lost to any war.

Being around so many young men like myself caused me to soon lose focus of my original objective. Through our evening exchanges of street tales in the barracks, the melodic song of the streets began to call to me anew. I was once again beginning to dance to its music. Going into the military only served to interrupt my drug use momentarily. I continued to use whatever drug I could get my hands on, mostly marijuana and alcohol while in boot camp in Fort Knox, Kentucky.

My advanced individual training was spent in Fort Sam Houston, in San Antonio, Texas. Being that close to Mexico gave my cronies and me access to a fairly potent grade of brown heroin we called Mexican Mud. While stationed in Texas, I used heroin quite frequently along with my fellow GI junkies from other large cities such as New York, Philadelphia, Houston, and New Orleans. Wherever I was stationed we somehow managed to find each other. At Fort Sam I was trained to become an army medic. The class on administering shots and starting IVs was a joke for those of us who were IV drug users. We knew more about finding and hitting veins than our instructors.

For a brief time after medic training I was stationed in Fort Riley, Kansas. This was the most desolate place I have ever seen in my life. On many occasions I sat in the window of my barracks which was located on Custer Hill and watched tumbleweeds roll by. I totally hated it there. There was nothing to do. There was absolutely no nightlife there. There were no single women for the men to socialize with. The only town close to Fort Riley was Junction City, Kansas. In Junction City the bars were filled with low-class prostitutes who had for the most part come there from other places around the country in order to hustle the GIs. The only attractions on post were wholesome activities. I wasn't into *wholesome* at this juncture in my life any more than I was into paying cheap prostitutes for sex. I used less drugs while in Fort Riley than in any other place I was stationed simply because there were none there to be had.

My unit was a part of the First Infantry Division, also known as the Big Red One. Army insiders also sometimes referred to this division as the "bloody red one" because of its history. I was told that the Big Red One had experienced bloody battles in all of the recent wars, including Vietnam. Many of the men in our company had recently been rotated back to the States from Vietnam. I learned from my friend and squad leader, John Hackleberry, whom everyone called Hack, of the bloody battles he and his comrades had waged in Nam. Hack, also a medic, told me that when the bullets and bombs began to fly he would duck behind his armored personnel carrier. Afraid to lift his head to take aim at an enemy, he raised his M-16 over his head, firing his weapon over the top of the vehicle in the direction of those assaulting his outfit.

Often as he recounted these tales to me his eyes would widen and beads of sweat would form on his forehead and nose. Once while working in the motor pool, a tank backfired, making a loud bang. I looked around and Hack was crawling around on the ground donning the same expression on his face he had when relating tales of the war. I had never witnessed a shell-shock episode before. I knew that he had been terrified during his thriteen-month stay in the war.

Interacting with Hack and others from the war let me see a glimpse of how devastatingly this awful war had affected the psyches of the men and women who served in it. There were men in my company that I was sure would never be able to function in society again. Many of these men sought drug-induced states of euphoria as an escape from their gruesome memories. Being around them made me glad that my foolish wish to be sent to Vietnam had not been granted.

For a moment my military career began to flourish. My sergeant noted that I possessed leadership potential. He was the first person to ever make that observation of me. I had no idea what he was talking about. I had never to that point envisioned myself as anyone's leader. However, this insightful sergeant assured me that I did possess this quality, and he began to nurture it. He began to give me leadership assignments over the other privates. He, no doubt, had plans to promote me to a higher rank whenever I became eligible. Had I remained in Fort Riley, I may have actually completed my second objective of having a successful military career. It was even hard for me to get into trouble in a place like that. However, a successful military career would never be mine.

In the spring of 1973 I was summoned to the administrative building of my post. The clerk called me to the glass-enclosed window. "Williams, how would you like to be transferred to West Germany?" he asked. I couldn't believe it. I had been trying to get transferred to Europe, somewhere, ever since I arrived in desolate Fort Riley. I dreamed of it often. Previously I had been told that no transfer was possible. "Yes, yes, I would love to be transferred to Germany," I gleefully told the clerk. "I'll go anywhere to get out of this place," I offered. "Well, that's good," he flatly stated. "Because you are going whether you like it or not."

Harold had been stationed in West Germany. He had told me many stories about all the enjoyable times he had had there. While stationed there he even traveled around to other parts of Europe. Plenty of frauleins and fine wine would soon be mine, I thought. The other reason I wanted to go to West Germany was that it is in direct proximity to France. In those days poppies were grown in Asia and processed into raw opium. The opium was then transported to Marseilles, France. In Marseilles, the opium was processed into high-grade heroin and shipped to other parts of the world. Remember *The French Connection* with Gene Hackman? I did. My plans included going to Marseilles, making my own French connection, shipping the drugs back to my brothers for safekeeping, and making a ton of money when my term in the army expired. Oh baby! This was it—my ticket to big money. I was on my way to the top now for sure. Actually, I was on my way to prison but didn't have the sense enough to know it.

I arrived in Germany in the spring of 1973. After a brief stay in the processing center at Frankfurt, I was sent to my permanent duty station in southwestern Germany. I was attached to a field artillery unit. My unit maintained the Pershing Missiles that were probably aimed at the USSR.

As I sat on the steps of my new home checking out my surroundings, four young black men, obviously enlisted men like myself, approached the doorway from across the parade field. "What's happenin', brother?" the shortest of all the men inquired. He extended his fist to me in an effort to offer me some "dap." Dap is a handshake practiced by many young blacks even today that originated in the army in the late 1960s.

Legend has it that it began in Vietnam by a young black man whose nickname was Dap. Dap, I was told, was short for the word dapper. He obviously was considered a sharp dresser. Dap, it is said, was a man who was very concerned about black unity. In Vietnam, blacks felt isolated, being so far from home and the support of their community. Most blacks faced some type of racism in the military, either subtle or overt. Because of this, there was a greater sense of solidarity among blacks overseas in the army than in the States. As a sign of unity, Dap invented a special handshake that he only taught to other blacks. Every black man who wished to show his commitment to black solidarity was expected to learn and practice dapping with other blacks. Dap, as the legend goes, was killed in Vietnam. So, engaging in this greeting was a tribute to him as well as a show of black unity. This custom confused and frustrated whites in the army to no end. They did not understand the concept.

Dap handshakes often involved knocking of fist, slapping of palms and several types of handshakes combined into one dap. More elaborate versions of dap might last for nearly five minutes. As this young man offered his fist to me I was unable to respond, as I did not know the dap of that region. I stretched forth my fist in an awkward attempted to follow him. Seeing that I did not know the dap, one of the other young men grasped my right wrist and guided me through the handshake. Each man offered me his fist in succession.

"You just gettin' here, blood?" inquired the man who had first greeted me. (Blood was short for youngblood, a common term of endearment among black men.)

"Yeah, I just got in last night from Frankfurt," I responded. "Where you from?" asked one young man I later learned was Rolland G. McCracken, from Chicago, whom everyone called Crack. "I'm from Detroit," I declared with pride. I had learned shortly after entering the army that people from Detroit were regarded with a certain sense of awe. Soldiers from Detroit apparently had earned a reputation for being streetwise and tough. Even my sergeants in boot camp singled me out, showing me unusual respect after learning I was from Detroit. I would ride this for all it was worth.

"Ohhh, Bosley, you got you a homey," Crack grinned to the shorter man who had initially greeted me. Richie Bosley, it turned out, was from Battle Creek, Michigan. A wide grin also swept across Bosley's face as he realized he had made contact with someone from close to home. Battle Creek is over a hundred miles from Detroit

109

and culturally is quite different, but it was close enough for us to be considered homies. In the military, being someone's homey or homeboy meant a lot. It meant that you were expected to hang out and look out for each other's well being. It also meant that you should watch each other's back. For you would likely end up life-long friends. So we were both happy to greet each other as homies.

Being a homey from Detroit gained me an invitation to Bosley's room, where the group was headed before they stopped to greet me. Bosley had managed to acquire more personal space than any soldier I had previously known. He occupied a major portion of a large bay that must have originally been meant to hold at least thirty soldiers. This army post was originally built to house the German Army. It was used by the Nazis during World War II and was larger than was needed for our relatively small field artillery company. So a man, if savvy enough, could arrange for a generous portion of space for himself. Bosley may have been short in stature, but he was far from being short on savvy.

We were stationed in a town by the name of Schwäbisch Gmünd, a very charming small city about sixty kilometers from Stuttgart. Stuttgart was a fairly big city like Detroit. In Stuttgart were all the attractions I found desirable. This would soon become my hangout.

Bosley's area was as elaborately furnished and decorated as any apartment I had been in. Apparently, my homey was a man of some means. He had a stereo component system that anyone would envy, along with an impressive collection of music. There were even several easy chairs in his area in which his guests could relax. Over his bed hung a poster of Angela Davis with the words "Free Angela."

Bosley's roommate was a man by the name of Freddie Haygood. Haygood, as we called him, was from Gary, Indiana, which is a stone's throw from Chicago. He and Crack were considered home-boys, even though Crack often jokingly ridiculed Gary as being a hick town. Haygood was a sort of quiet guy who liked to use most-ly the softer drugs and tried to stay out of any real trouble. The other man who had accompanied us to the room, I learned, was a Puerto Rican from New Jersey named Mario. His skin was about as dark as mine. He did not speak Spanish and he hung out with the black guys. Most people assumed he was black. Also, I later learned that Mario had a learning disability. This disability hampered him from learning Spanish, as his grandfather would have liked him to. His inability to speak Spanish made him a black sheep in his grandfather's eyes. He was quite dejected at being shunned by one from whom he desperately craved approval, making him a prime candidate for substance abuse.

Crack had been a gangbanger before he left Chicago for military service. His joining the army was a direct result of some gang-related trouble he had gotten into back home. Like me, Crack came into the army hoping to avoid prison. Also like me, he was not doing a very good job at it. He had no problem inflicting pain on other human beings. In fact, I believe he quite enjoyed it.

It was quite apparent that though he was much smaller in stature than the other men, Bosley was the undisputed leader of this group. He possessed a street cunning and understanding of human nature that gave him an advantage over the rest. His leadership was not based on physical dominance and intimidation, as is often the case in crime circles, but rather on benevolence and charisma. Anyone who needed money, drugs, an encouraging word, or most any other kind of favor could usually depend on Bosley. Once granted a favor, though, one could always be sure that one day he would call upon you to repay it.

We five sat in Bosley's room feeling each other out. Through coded language only understood by drug users, we learned that we had a common love for drugs. After informally interviewing me, a checking of my pedigree, so to speak, Bosley and the others were confident that I was one of them, an assumed wolf. He casually reached over to his stash to retrieve a "turd" of hashish wrapped in plastic wrap. Breaking off a chunk of what I was told was Lebanese Blond hashish, he crumbled it and placed it into a small water pipe. This was my first time seeing hashish. The pipe passed from man to man, each holding a Bic lighter over the bowl of the pipe to keep it burning. Soon I was feeling the effects of the drug, as was everyone else. Passing the pipe among us made all considerably looser.

We talked for a while as the group took the opportunity to get to know me better. After about an hour of talking, smoking, and drinking wine, for some reason Bosley felt comfortable enough with my presence to go deeper into his stash. This time when he drew out his hand, it contained a small plastic bag of white powder.

"This is the real deal here, homeboy," he assured me. He took an album cover from his shelf and began to break up the caked-up powder with a thin plastic card, a ritual with which I was well familiar. Instead of passing the board around for us to sniff the heroin, he picked up his pack of cigarettes. Working the filtered part of the cigarette between his index finger and his thumb, Bosley loosened the filter until he was able to pull it out of the cigarette in one piece. He then removed a portion of the tobacco in the same manner. Using the card, he dumped a small quantity of the heroin into the cigarette, working it down through as much of the tobacco as he could. He then lit the cigarette and handed it to me. "Smoke it like you would a joint of weed," he instructed me.

Continuing to follow Bosley's instructions, I was amazed at the potency of the heroin. A few puffs and I was as high as if I had injected some of Detroit's most potent heroin directly into my veins. Could it be that I had so quickly found the French connection?

As we became more intimate over the next few weeks, the group began to share with me some of the ways they made their money. Their crafts included selling black market items such as cigarettes and liquor to the Germans, boosting (stealing from department stores), trafficking in drugs, and armed and unarmed robbery. Some members of the group that I did not meet the first day were Deuce and Macey. Deuce was a street-slick fellow from Baltimore. He was a sneak thief who would steal the gold fillings from his own grandmother's teeth. Macey was from Miami. He was a hulk of a man standing about 6'3" and weighing all of 260 pounds. His skin was dark and rough. Macey was a mean-spirited individual who, like Crack, enjoyed inflicting pain on others.

I learned that about a week before I arrived at my new assignment Bosley, Crack, Macey, and Deuce had robbed a French drug dealer. Bosley had met this man on one of his trips to Marseilles. He had arranged for the Frenchman to smuggle a substantial quantity of heroin into Germany. The Frenchman met Bosley, hoping to exchange the drugs for a large amount of American money. Instead, this entire crew of American thugs robbed him, beating him mercilessly in the process. The way the encounter was described to me, it was as violent as any I have ever heard of. The Frenchman was seen near the post looking for Bosley for some time after the incident. Unable to find him, he sent Bosley a message by another GI that he would surely kill Bosley and his crew for what they had done.

These men had surely risked their very lives by robbing this French drug dealer. They stashed the drugs so they could not be found in any of their possession. One day Bosley went to the stash and found the bundle of drugs and the money they had made from selling some of it gone—vanished without a trace. After a meeting of the four of them, the suspicion fell on Deuce. Crack pounced upon Deuce like a jaguar and beat him unrelentingly. "Open the window," Crack growled at the others. "I'm throwing this   out the window," he swore. He dragged Deuce by his neck over to the window. "I'm killing you right now, punk," Crack promised Deuce. "Please don't kill me," pleaded Deuce. "I got the stuff hid. I will go and get it and bring it to you," Deuce assured. Picking him up from the open window and flinging him toward the door by his neck, Crack instructed Deuce to go and get the money and drugs. Not one speck or dollar had better be missing, threatened Crack. At lightening speed, Deuce lit from the room and was back in an instant with the precious package. All were happy after that. Even Deuce was happy to yet be in possession of his miserable life. I decided at that time that Crack was a person I wanted as a friend and never as an enemy.

I worked in the medical clinic in the daytime. This clinic provided the medical treatment for all the army personnel and their dependents assigned to my base. My job as a medic was similar to that of a nurse. Because I was so good at my craft, I eventually was given the responsibility to treat my own burn patients, which is a serious responsibility. I administered shots to men, women, and even babies. I was a whiz at suturing, it turned out. I even participated in some minor surgical procedures. The doctors who ran the clinic were very impressed with my skills. I had the best surgical technique they had seen in a young medic, they said. My future in the medical field could be bright according to them. Hey, I was already in the pharmaceutical field, why not? I enjoyed an elevated status among my peers because I was the only black medic attached to my unit. I must say I was quite striking in my medical whites. The Germans in the community had no frame of reference for my position, so they referred to me as "Herr Doktor." Hey Mamma, I made it!

My evenings and weekends were a different story altogether. In the evening I hung out with my crew—actually Bosley's crew. I went to Stuttgart every chance I got. Bosley introduced me to a club called the White Horse. The White Horse was located in the red-light district of Stuttgart. There I met many other young men like myself who were stationed all over that region of West Germany. We all came to the White Horse looking for the same thing: drugs, women, and a quick dollar, or deutsche mark. We took those too.

We engaged in a wide range of crimes. I was learning the ropes from the best in West Germany. I trafficked in drugs, boosted from stores, and robbed other drug dealers in order to support my growing heroin habit. Because the drugs were so powerful, our tolerance for the drug increased rapidly, requiring more and more of it for us to get high. Soon smoking the potent powder was not good enough to satisfy us. We began to intravenously inject the liquefied drug.

Bosley was at the end of his tour of duty. Time came for him to leave the military. He promised that he would come back to Germany as soon as he got his passport and was able to return. Actually, there were many young black men who had done the same. They found a sense of freedom in Germany they did not enjoy back at home. The Germans were not nearly as prejudiced as the whites in the States. The German officials had no experience in dealing with street-slick, young black men. Therefore, we gained a false sense of security, believing that we were so clever we could not be caught.

Bosley remained true to his word. He was rotated back to the States and honorably discharged from the army. He was back in Germany in about two months with tales of the horror of his experience back home. His physical system was so used to the nearly pure level of heroin we were using that he found it impossible to get high on any amount of street drugs in Michigan. He had sent a considerable amount of money back home while in Germany. He spent it all in a short period of time trying to chase the elusive high he had gotten so accustomed to in Germany. Finally, all his money spent, he borrowed money from his aunt for a plane ticket back to Germany. He was not the same Bosley, though.

No longer being in the army, Bosley was no longer able to hustle the way he had as a soldier. Consequently, he had a hard time making money. He quickly became reduced to scrounging for drugs at the White Horse or anywhere else. This meant also that all of our lifestyles suffered a drastic turn downwards. After all, Bosley had been our leader. He had always come up with lucrative ways to attain cash. Now that he was struggling, we all struggled.

I managed to acquire an apartment from a woman who was an Australian national. She had been living in Germany for some time. A black GI had promised to marry her and take her back to the States. Therefore, she needed someone to take over her lease. I conned the apartment manager into thinking that I was a sergeant, because enlisted men were not allowed to live off post. I took over her lease and Bosley lived in the apartment with me. With the apartment as our base of operation, our hustle slowly began to get better.

Bosley had somehow acquired a pistol that he rented to a number of us who wanted to pull armed robberies for a cut of our take. Our favorite low-risk scheme was to pose as drug dealers wanting to sell large quantities of hashish to drug dealers at the white version of the White Horse called the Lido Club. We advertised that we sold kilos and up. A kilo of hashish cost one thousand dollars. If someone expressed an interest in doing business with us, we knew they had at least a thousand dollars. I wanted to make some fast cash, so I asked Bosley to give me the gun. Another regular at the White Horse named Carl also wanted to make a fast buck, so we agreed to team up going to the Lido together.

We targeted white GIs for robberies and other abuses for a number of reasons. First, we knew that we could not get away with sticking up black GIs without facing some kind of retaliation. We felt that since we experienced racism and discrimination at home and racism in the military, we were justified in our dislike toward whites. There was no way we could get at those who were the real source of the racism, so we victimized those whites closest to us. Also, we knew that most whites could not fight as well as we could since we grew up thumping in the streets. Lastly, we did it because we were thieves. I realize how wrong it was for us to target them the way we did. No one is ever justified in targeting another person simply because of the color of his or her skin.

We found a guy who wanted to purchase two kilos of hashish. This meant that he had at least two thousand dollars. We successfully relieved him of his wad of money and made it back to the White Horse without being caught. As the club was closing for the night, Bosley and I prepared to go to the train station for the trip back home. A couple of military detectives who were a part of the army's Criminal Investigation Division (CID) walked into the club with the man who I had earlier robbed. He quickly identified me as the person who had robbed him. I was arrested and taken to the MP station, charged with armed robbery.

The MPs turned me over to my company commander in the morning. The commanding officer restricted me to post to await trial. This meant that I was not able to continue to live in the apartment. A sergeant who was assigned to me took me by the apartment to gather my things. Bosley, thankfully, was at the apartment. I handed Bosley the money I had left from the robbery. For some reason, the detectives only counted the money and allowed me to keep it instead of taking it as evidence. I had about $800 left. "Get me a lawyer, man," I instructed Bosley. "I am in real trouble. They are giving me a general court-martial," I informed him. A general court-martial is the highest form of military justice, which was nearly always used in felony cases. I was afraid if convicted I would face serving time not only in military prison, but it would also be discovered that I was on the run from Detroit and be sent to state prison when I finished my military sentence. Bosley assured me he would take care of everything as he had always done.

Being restricted to post was very difficult for me. It meant I was no longer free to move about to acquire money for my substantial heroin habit. I could not expect others like Crack to carry me for long. About two days into my restriction, I asked Crack to go to the apartment to check on the progress that Bosley had made in attaining my lawyer. Crack came back with an expression on his face that I knew did not mean good news. "Bosley is gone, Joe. He took the money you gave him and bought a plane ticket back home," Crack managed to relate to me.

Sitting there in absolute disbelief, hours passed before the truth of Crack's revelation sunk in. My best friend, my homey, no less, had turned tail and left me in my greatest hour of need. Surely there was no hope for me to stay out of prison now.

8

THREE
STRIKES

A lthough only early fall and still fairly warm outside, I lay shivering under my thick army blanket. It felt strange and unnatural being so cold on the inside, yet perspiring profusely. My legs and arms ached to the bone; yet no amount of rubbing and massaging would relieve even a fraction of the pain. A large snake crawled around in my bowels causing my stomach to constantly churn. Periodically, this tortuous creature would make his way up my lanky body, bursting past my pasty tongue, spewing his foul venom into the plastic bucket at my bedside, only to retreat back into the recesses of my gut. I had been in this sorrowful state for a number of days. The doctors at the clinic fired me from my job at the clinic after learning of my substance abuse. I was not trained to perform any other task, so I was not missed by anyone as I lay in my room. The first stage of heroin withdrawal normally lasts about a week before the person begins to feel human again. I was only at the halfway point of the first week. There was yet plenty of hell to come.

As dangerous as cold turkey withdrawal may have been, admitting being deeply addicted to heroin and checking into the junkie ward at the military hospital was not viewed as a viable option. One did not voluntarily turn himself in to the authorities unless death was imminent. Thankfully, the wakeful moments of withdrawal periodically gave way to unconsciousness and half-consciousness. While in this state, I felt a tugging at my arm. Faint voices sounded familiar, but yet unrecognizable. Were these sensations real or merely a form of dopefiend delirium? Now a prick in my arm! My eyes slowly focused to distinguish the shadowy figures hovering over my bed. It was Crack and Skip. Skip was Crack's protégé. He was a silly acting young soldier from Virginia whom Crack had taken under his wing. Skip's stock-in-trade was boosting. He was as good at it as any I have known. He seemed to really look up to Crack, seeking constant direction and approval from him.

Slowly I began to feel much better. The pain in my legs and arms was subsiding. The snake in my gut was steadily becoming lifeless. Sitting up on my elbows, I began to realize that these two *angels of mercy* had come into the room while I was knocked out to deliver an early Christmas present. They had administered a shot of heroin into my limp body without waking me so as not to cause me further misery. Words cannot even begin to express the gratitude I felt about this great act of benevolence by my friends. I would return the favor on several occasions.

Since I had been out of commission and Bosley had escaped back to the US, the post had been quite dry. Usually, it had been one of us that had gone to Stuttgart to purchase drugs and bring them back to the post. Crack and Skip had been successful in locating a small amount of the drug. Everyone in our circle felt extremely sorrowful over the predicament I was in. They all knew how I felt about Bosley. Crack had tried quite unsuccessfully on a few occasions to shake me out of the state of depression into which I had fallen. Once more he would try his pep talk in an attempt to help me think through my problems.

"Joe, you gotta get yourself together, brother," Crack encouraged. "You have caught some bad breaks, but you shouldn't be thinking about giving up. I watched you since you been here and I know you a sharp brother. You can beat this if you put your mind to it," he continued. The compassion and caring he and Skip had demonstrated toward me earned him my full attention. Bosley's treachery had rocked my faith in friendship. Now these two men had gone out of their way to show me that a sense of charity still remained in the world, even within a circle of thieves and drug addicts. This show of love and concern touched me in a way that few in life ever have. I am sorry to say it, but the greatest moments of encouragement in my life have not come from Christians, but from "criminals."

Crack's message of hope began to sink into my heart. I believed his words. Perhaps my situation was not as hopeless as I had led myself to believe. After Crack and Skip left the room, I got up, showered, changed clothes, put clean linens on my bed, and began to think through my issues. There was nothing that could be done about Bosley. He was long gone along with my money. I began to see that I had been charged with a serious crime; however, I had not yet been convicted. The possibility still existed that I could some-how beat this case.

I observed my restriction to post for about three weeks. A way had to be found to get off post undetected so that I could begin to prepare for my day in court. Also, I felt I had a responsibility to my fellow drug addicts to get back on my job of supplying the post with drugs.

Getting off post was even easier than I expected. The guard posted at the gate never even gave me a second look. To him I was just another GI coming and going. It was off to Stuttgart. The strat-egy I developed to beat the pending court marshal was to insist that there had been a mistaken identity. I was not the one who had robbed the white soldier. I was not even close to the area where he was robbed on that night. Now, I must find witnesses to make my alibi sound credible. Crack and Skip agreed to testify falsely on my behalf. That was well and good, but they were my known associ-ates. They would be expected to stick up for me. I needed someone more credible than they.

I had begun to date a German girl from Stuttgart named Elena Rau. She was a very attractive young woman who hung out at the White Horse. She possessed an innocent beauty. It was months after we began to date that I learned the secret of her youthful look. She was only seventeen years old. Though I was only twenty-one at the time, I was not accustomed to dating girls that young. However, her age did not present a problem in her country, either legally or socially. Elena was not a drug user, but for some reason liked hanging out at this club. She lived about three kilometers from the White Horse in an old house with her grandfather whom she referred to as Opah. I had gone to her house to visit on several occasions but never felt quite comfortable there. Opah was a World War II veteran, which in my ignorant mind made him a Nazi. Surely he could not relish the idea of his young granddaughter dating a black American. To him it must have brought flashbacks of Joe Louis and Jesse Owens. Also, I reasoned that he probably had an old Luger or hand grenade hidden somewhere around that old house just in case of trouble. I gave Opah a very wide berth.

Elena and I had not seen each other since my arrest. Someone who was at the club that night had told her what had happened. However, she did not know how to check on my status. We were very happy to see each other. She probably thought that she would never see me again. There were many times during that three weeks I was sure I would never see her again. Explaining my situation to her, I asked Elena if she would testify falsely at my hearing. The hearing was to determine whether there was enough evidence to hold me over for trial. Elena agreed to the deception. It never entered into my selfish mind how wrong it was for me to do such a thing.

Being back at the White Horse was great. I socialized for a while, catching up on the happenings since I had been away. As I stood by the hallway, which led to the restrooms, I was engaged in a conversation with a guy that we called Slim Jay. Jay was from Oakland, California, and had been a very successful GI drug dealer a number of years earlier. Like many others, he had returned to Germany thinking he would continue his lucrative trade. And like many others, he found that once he was out of the military, it was difficult to continue dealing drugs as he had previously. His lifestyle had deteriorated considerably since returning to Germany. Jay lived with his German wife and child in Stuttgart. He engaged in whatever kind of hustle or odd job he could find in the daytime. At night he usually hung out at the White Horse looking for a cheap or free heroin high.

Jay was also known for tagging others with catchy monikers. Watching as I stood in the entrance of the hallway he commented that I had the demeanor of a killer. "What's your name, youngblood?" he inquired. "My name is Joe," I answered. "You look like a stone killer standing there. From now on your name is going to be Joe Killer," he informed me. The others standing around agreed that this was a name that suited me. Although I never killed anyone, I attempted to carry myself as if I would do it without much thought. This was actually my strategy to keep from killing or hurting anyone, or from being hurt or killed myself. I liked this moniker as well. It stuck.

Using the military pay I had received earlier that day, I purchased all the heroin my money would buy. I would then take the heroin back to base, mix it to stretch the quantity by diluting the potency, and then sell it to the others on base. This would allow my bankroll to quickly grow. With no hitches I would be able to purchase larger and larger quantities of the drug, assuring that our base would once again have an abundance of the tragically magical powder. In the initial stages of this plan, I would need to make frequent trips to Stuttgart. Without realizing it, I had filled the leadership void left by Bosley. For some reason unknown to me, the others were perfectly willing to follow my lead.

Still I needed another witness to complete my alibi. This time I went to Maggie. Maggie was a beautiful, willowy, olive-toned German girl who lived in Schwäbisch Gmünd. We had been friends since the first week I arrived in Germany. Maggie agreed to testify that I was at her house the evening of the robbery until a certain time. Crack and Skip would back up Maggie's story by testifying they were there with me. After I left Maggie's house, the alibi went, I caught the train to Stuttgart to visit Elena until a time that would have made it impossible for me to be on the other side of town robbing the victim.

A JAG (Judge Advocate General) lawyer was assigned to my

defense. This is the army's version of a court-appointed lawyer. Captain Jacobson was nobody's slouch, though. This shrewd young lawyer from southern Florida took an instant liking to me. Captain Jacobson, I could tell, was a very good man. He truly believed in justice for the little fellow. He was no doubt a liberal who believed that black people nearly always received the short end of the stick. He was going to make certain that I was one black person who received favorable treatment in the courtroom. Whether or not he actually bought my story is unknown. He liked it enough, however, to use it as a defense, unaltered.

The day of the hearing finally came. Having never been involved in such a proceeding, I had no idea what to expect. If bound over for trial and later convicted, I faced certain prison time. Before the trial, I went to the post barbershop and had the barber fit me with the most military-looking haircut he had in his repertoire. I stepped into the hearing room sporting a crisply pressed dress-green uniform, spit-shined shoes and all. I was even impressed with myself.

Instead of a real judge, an army officer was appointed to hear my case. As it turned out, these officers, though having no formal legal training, served on a rotating basis, hearing evidence related to all levels of offenses. These officers would make the determination to bind a case over for court-martial or to dismiss the charges.

The officer assigned to my hearing possessed a somewhat oafish demeanor. His deportment seemed to apologize for assuming such an important role. Captain Jacobson sized him up the moment he walked into the room. He had guys like this for lunch with room for dessert.

The prosecution called the victim to the stand. He offered a very weak version of the events that transpired that night, desperately attempting not to acknowledge that he had come to the club to purchase drugs. He had no witnesses. Of course, none of his friends would ever admit that they were at a club known for drug trafficking. From the witness stand he identified me as the one who had robbed him. In his cross-examination, Captain Jacobson destroyed his testimony as well as his credibility.

I was called to the stand to tell my story. I wove a skillful yarn insisting that I had been nowhere near the Lido on the night in question. I had been at Maggie's apartment, then on to Elena's, but never was I at the Lido. Crack and Skip swore on the Bible that what I had said was in fact true. Then Maggie and Elena were ushered into the courtroom. They were dressed to the nines looking exceptionally stunning. I had never seen either of them look so lovely. The jaw of the officer overseeing the case dropped as they entered the courtroom. He was obviously taken with their beauty. He would have easily believed anything that came out of their mouths. "Yes, it is true," they both agreed. I had followed the exact timeline Captain Jacobson and I described in my defense. The case against me was dismissed.

Crack was right! All I had to do was to put my mind to it. After nearly two months of anxiety, I was again a free man. However, although my charges had been dismissed for lack of evidence, the officers and non-commissioned officers in my unit had enough evidence to convince themselves that I was not the kind of soldier they wanted in their outfit. They became determined to make sure that I did not receive an honorable discharge from the army. If they had anything to do with it, before I got out of the army, I would indeed serve the prison sentence I had so narrowly escaped.

About a month after my charges were dismissed, while in my room, I heard a key turning in my door lock. At that time, I did not have a roommate, so I knew that this was not a friendly visit. I was lying on my bunk reading a comic book when the visitors arrived. My first sergeant, whom everyone referred to as Top, entered the room first. Coming into the door behind Top were two individuals whom I recognized as local CID officers.

They asked me where I had hidden my stash of drugs. "Top, you know I don't use drugs no more," I appealed to my first sergeant. "Willie, just tell them what they want to know," Top replied. Top was the only person in life who ever called me Willie, obviously his nickname for Williams, as soldiers are always known by their last names. I did not like being called Willie, but went along with it if it meant that Top had some kind of affection toward me—

anything that might provide me with a psychological edge.

The two detectives ordered me to open my locker. Interestingly, they went straight to the spot where I had been keeping my stash. Fortunately for me, though, I had decided to move my stash to a new hiding place just that morning. The drugs were rolled up in a pair of thick military socks and placed into my dirty laundry bag. The detectives seemed baffled when they did not find the drugs in my locker. They continued to search my room, never even looking at the laundry bag. My cooker with heroin residue still in it and part of a syringe, however, were found. I was handcuffed behind my back and taken to the MP station, charged with possession of drug paraphernalia and *drug residue,* barely more than a misdemeanor charge. I was again scheduled to be court-martialed. This time I was to have a special court-martial, which is not nearly as serious as the general court-martial I had faced earlier.

Captain Jacobson informed me that the MPs had gotten some-one close to me to inform on me. Apparently, that is why the detectives went right to the place where I normally hid my drugs. They thought they had me, but once again it seemed that I had dodged a bullet. Captain Jacobson assured me that I had nothing to worry about when I went to trial. He accused the officers in my company of singling me out for harassment. Boy, was he good!

Continuing my drug trafficking activities, I began to believe that since the MPs had failed in two attempts to nab me that I was just too clever for them. These hick police could never catch a street-smart guy like me. My term in the army was drawing to an end. Even though I had failed in my desire to amass the large quantity of heroin for shipment back home, it looked as though I would at least make it out of the military with an honorable discharge.

Bosley had the audacity to come back to Germany. This time he was staying with some friends in Stuttgart. His reputation in Schwäbisch Gmünd was shot after everyone learned how he had left me to twist in the wind. I had told myself that if ever given the opportunity I would shoot him, stab him, beat him, or all of the above. After seeing the pitiful condition to which he had sunk, I could only muster up feelings of disgust and pity for him. So quickly he had become little more than a bum whom few people trusted.

I made it through the winter with no further trouble with the military authorities. By March of 1974 it had become harder and harder to acquire drugs, making it difficult for me to stay supplied. General Keys, the commander of the Fifth Army, had declared war on drugs. The Vietnam War had ended while I was stationed in Kansas. The new enemy, it seemed, was my junkie friends and me. How ironic it seemed to be a part of the military whose purpose it was to fight America's enemies and to be considered its enemy as well.

Things had gotten quite dry around the post. I was having difficulty maintaining enough drugs to sell and use. I had begun to more frequently supplement my drug income by pulling both armed and unarmed robberies. Crack and I terrorized any white GIs who mistakenly thought they could sell drugs on our post. We robbed practically any we found. We wrongly rationalized that since we faced racism in the army it was all right to victimize white GIs. One of Dad's favorite sayings was that people don't get mad enough to steal. They steal because they are thieves.

Since my own cash was short, a number of other drug users pooled their money, giving it to me to go to Stuttgart to buy drugs and bring them back to the post. I was the only one, it seemed, who knew the drill. I took Smiley Holland with me. Slim Jay had given him the moniker Smiley because he smiled all the time. Because of his incessant grin, it was usually difficult to know exactly what was on Smiley's mind.

Smiley and I followed the same routine I had observed for nearly a year since arriving in Germany. We caught the train from Schwäbisch Gmünd to Stuttgart, going straight to the White Horse. Things were uncharacteristically slow in the club. General Key's war strategy was truly having its desired effect, it seemed. None of my usual contacts were in the club that night. I ended up purchasing drugs from a man I did not know very well, only to learn afterward the drugs were of a very low quality. It would be quite disappointing for me to return to post with only these poor quality drugs, having spent most of the money I had arrived with.

There was a dice game going on in the back hallway of the club.

I hoped that I could somehow get in the game and multiply the small amount of money I had left. Never having been particularly skilled in gambling of any kind, the remaining money I had was soon gone. The prospect of returning to post with drugs that weren't worth anything and no money was depressing. Yet the club was about to close, so Smiley and I reluctantly decided to leave and head back.

As we were leaving, a British man who was in town on business approached me. He had earlier seen me talking to some of the girls at the bar and mistook me for a pimp. He was looking to have a good time with one of the girls and asked if I could help him. I told him that those girls were not prostitutes. However, I knew of a place where he could find what he was looking for. I would be happy to take him there.

Smiley and I agreed among ourselves to lead him to a secluded spot where we planned to relieve him of all of his money. This gullible individual would be the answer to our immediate financial problems. We led him like a sheep to the slaughter. We took him to an underground passage that we know of which was on the way to the train station. Once we got him to the spot where no one else was around, Smiley, who was about 6'1" and about 190 pounds, would grab him, pinning his arms behind his back. I would then punch him in the stomach as hard as I could. Hopefully this would leave him incapacitated. We would take his money and continue to the train station and back to base.

The plan seemed to be working to perfection. He, blinded by lust, stupidly followed us down into the underground passage. Smiley grabbed him and I punched him. Reaching into his suit jacket, I removed his wallet. Just then, two men entered the under-ground passage. Seeing what we were up to, they began to call for the German police. The German police had a fearsome reputation among criminals. They were known to shoot first and ask questions later. They were also known for brutally subduing their suspects.

Smiley and I ran out of the other end of the passage and onto the streets. The two men ran behind us, continuing to call for the police. We split up agreeing to meet at the train station. We had not planned to rob anyone when we left, so I was wearing a pair of shoes with no back on them called clogs. These shoes did not allow me to run at full speed. Also, physically I was in terrible condition. The hard drugs, cigarettes, wine, and hard life I had lived for the past year had taken its toll on me. I knew I would not be able to run for long. I ducked down an alley in a last-ditch attempt to shake my pursuer. It didn't work. Instead, he closed in on me. As he was about to overtake me, I spun around and punched him in the face. We both were breathing heavily and were tired. He was a shorter and stouter man than I. Realizing that he would not be successful at boxing me he decided to rush me, pinning me to a chain-link fence. He pinned my slim body to the fence, holding on to the chain link for support with his fingers. I punched him furiously about his body in an attempt to free myself. By now, however, my punches had little power.

In a brief moment, I saw a German police officer running around the corner shouting commands to me that I did not understand. In his hand was some type of submachine gun. I raised my hands high over my head, showing the officer and everyone else around that I offered no resistance to arrest.

Smiley arrived at the police station shortly after I had arrived. He was not smiling now. We were placed in separate cells until morning when we were taken before a German official. The German official explained to us that we would be bound over in a German court for our crime. We thought that he was bluffing in order to get us to confess to what we had done. Being ignorant of the agreement between the U.S. Armed Forces and West Germany, we believed that they had to turn us over to the American military officials. We would never confess, though, in any event. Instead, we wove a vicious lie, claiming that the man had made a homosexual pass at me, precipitating the beating.

That day we were transferred to a larger facility that must have been their city jail. From there we were taken straight to prison the next day. You see, in West Germany, as in most foreign countries, there is no concept of a person being innocent until proven guilty. A person is guilty until proven innocent. Also, there is no speedy trial system. A person could be in prison for several years before his trial is ever completed. Therefore, there was no holding facility such as the county jails in this country. I was shocked into reality as the van in which we were transported entered through the massive gates of the prison. We were provided with prison clothing, linens, and a set of tin dinnerware. This did not look good at all. It looked as if they expected us to be their guests for some time.

I sat in the office of the prison official wearing the ill-fitting blue prison uniform. He explained to me the seriousness of my charges. "Herr Villiams, because of the seriousness of your offense, the prosecutor will ask that you be sentenced to eight years," he informed me. "Because of your youthfulness, you qualify for a youthful offenders program. Through this program you will likely receive a sentence of only four years if you confess and show remorse for your crime. However, the prosecutor may appeal the decision and attempt to have you serve the entire eight years," he stated.

This official assured me that my case would not be turned over to the American authorities. According to the Status of Forces Agreement between the U.S. military and West Germany, the Germans, I was told, were able to select any case they wanted for prosecution in German court. Most cases were turned over to the Americans. However, my case had been selected for German prosecution.

By now my body was already experiencing relatively mild withdrawal symptoms. Listening to this man so matter-of-factly promise me that I would be spending the next four to eight years in a German prison greatly intensified my illness. My body doubled over. I leaned forward, almost falling from the chair. A huge knot formed in the pit of my stomach.

"What is the name of your lawyer?" the official asked. "Captain Jacobson," I managed to utter. "How do you spell his name?" he questioned further. I opened my mouth to respond to the question, but my brain had ceased to function properly. "J-o-b, no that's not right, j-a-b-o," I stammered. Seeing that I was obviously in a state of shock, the official called for the guard to take me to my cell.

9

LIKE
A MOTH

I was assigned to a one-person cell in the German prison. As I lay on the bed the words of the prison official continually rang in my head. The possibility of serving eight years was overwhelming. Could I even survive eight years in this place if it came down to it? The man in the cell next to me was an African who appeared to be quite mentally unstable. He had been in there for over two years and had not even been to court yet. What would I be like eight years from now, leaving this place, returning home to Detroit? I tried to imagine. Probably as crazy as a road lizard.

The cell to which I was assigned was quite bare. It didn't have bars like many American prisons have, but had a metal door with a slot through which the jailers could speak. Like a moth to the fire I had been drawn to this place. I had known for some time I would end up in some place like this. For some reason, it seemed that I could not help myself, stop myself from meeting with this inevitability. It was like an irresistible destiny for me, it seemed. I did nothing substantively to try to avoid it. Yet now that I was here it seemed so unbearable.

The only book in my room was a Bible. The problem was it was written in German. Elena had taught me to speak some German, although I could not read it at all. Picking up this once-familiar book, I opened it to the New Testament. Peering over the pages, the only two words I could make out were Mary and Jesus. Memories of church, Sunday school, and devotions with Mamma flooded my memory.

I was in a jam that no human would be able to help me out of. Mamma had taught me that when I was in trouble I should call on the Lord for help. Would God even listen to someone as wretched as I? Falling on my knees to the cold floor, I began to cry out to God. "God, I have done so much wrong," I began. "I have strayed so far away from You. Lord, I need Your help now," I prayed. "I know that I have done wrong and I must pay for it. But Lord, please get me out of this German prison and let me serve my time in Leavenworth where I will be closer to my family. I believe I will go crazy if I have to stay here for so long. Lord, if You will do that for me, I will change. I will stop doing the things I have been doing and go back to church," I bargained. "Amen."

The days slowly passed as I lay in my solitary cell having very little contact with the other inmates. Through brief encounters with others, I learned that there were twenty-one other blacks in that prison, mostly Americans. A major drug dealer I used to do business with at the White Horse was there. Also, I learned that this was the prison that confined the Badder Meinhauf Gang, a notorious group of German terrorists. Oh yeah, I had made it to the big time all right.

I lay on my bunk contemplating my fate when the intercom in my cell began to crackle. "Herr Villiams," the voice called in a thick German accent. "Get your things packed. You go home today, yah." This could not be true, I reasoned to myself. The German official had appeared quite serious in relating to me that this prison would be my home for some years to come. This was no doubt some kind of sick joke the guards were trying to play on me, and I was not going along with it. I remained still on my bunk.

I heard the key turning in my cell door. Surprised, I backed into the corner of my cell in preparation for what may be some kind of roughing up by the guards. Instead, a rather jocular guard bounced into my cell wearing a wide toothy grin. "Herr Villiams, is true. You going home today. Come, I help you get your things." How could this be? Stepping outside my cell, I was greeted by a now smiling Smiley Holland. Smiley already had on his street clothes. We hugged each other in joy, bouncing up and down. Neither of us knew what could have changed the official's mind.

As I walked down the hall on the way to secure my personal effects, the guard in the control room smiled and gave me a thumbs up. "Guten tag, Herr Villiams." They were happy for our good fortune. Then I saw the German official who had told me of my likely fate upon my arrival at the prison. I ran up to him and grabbed his hand and began shaking it wildly. "Thank you so much for changing your mind," I blurted out to him. This official looked back at me with a look of bewilderment. "I assure you, I had nothing to do with it," he said. Then I recalled the prayer I had prayed in my cell. Mamma was right. God truly does help you in your time of trouble.

We were turned over to the MPs for transportation back to our unit. The next day I was taken to Manheim stockade, which is a military version of a county jail, to await trial. For the first two months, although in the army jail, our case was still under German jurisdiction. The Germans still wanted badly to prosecute our case. There were about ten other soldiers in that facility that were also under what we called German hold. None of us were happy about it.

The military jailer stood at the door of my dormitory-style cell, informing me that my lawyer was here to see me. Happily, I jumped from my bunk and went to the door. Captain Jacobson sat in the attorney's room waiting for me to enter. His face had a serious, yet pleased expression. "Joe, I've got some good news for you today," he began. "I have been able to have your case turned over to the military," he continued. A great load was lifted from my shoulders upon hearing those wonderful words. As it turned out, the Germans were playing fast and loose with the Status of Forces Agreement. They were supposed to select the cases they wanted to try at random. They could not choose a certain category of crime such as murder or rape to categorically try in their courts. Captain

Jacobson had discovered that they had established a pattern of trying all the robbery cases, so they had to turn my case over to the military.

God really was answering my prayer. He had so wonderfully kept His part of the bargain. I broke my end of the deal shortly after being released from the German prison. Even while in the stockade, I was still getting high every chance I got. I still loved the criminal lifestyle and planned to return to it once released. I gave God absolutely no glory for what He had done for me. I gave my lawyer all the credit.

Smiley and I were offered a deal by the military. If we pled guilty to our crime, we would only have to serve one year in Fort Leavenworth prison. Most guys charged with the same crime were getting much stiffer sentences. Smiley's lawyer convinced him that it was a good deal, so he took it. I never had any luck gambling, so I reasoned that I had better take the deal as well. At our court-martial we were convicted, sentenced to two years of hard labor, and given a dishonorable discharge. Because of our pre-trial agreement we would only have to serve one year and receive a Bad Conduct Discharge.

Right as the court-martial ended, Captain Jacobson rushed into the courtroom. It was too late, though. It was all over. Given credit for the four months I had spent in the stockade, I would spend the next eight in prison. Captain Jacobson told me that he would have been able to win my case but was prevented from seeing me by his superiors. They even waylaid him so that he could not attend my trial. He was apparently very sad that I would be forced to suffer the degradation of prison. We shook hands one last time and said good-bye. I just couldn't figure out what it was that man saw in me that made him work so hard on my behalf. Obviously, he saw something in me that I was not able to see because of being blinded by my addiction, lifestyle, and ultimately Satan. God bless you, Captain Jacobson.

We traveled to Fort Leavenworth, Kansas, by plane, stopping over in Fort Dix, New Jersey, for one night. It was now July of 1974. The Kansas sun was blazing as our van entered the penitentiary. At the time I was there, Fort Leavenworth Prison had been in existence for well over a hundred years. It had been home to some of the most infamous prisoners in this country. While I was there, Lt. Calley, the defendant in the Me Lai massacre case, in which twenty-eight Vietnamese citizens were murdered and buried in a mass grave, was also a resident. Calley had killed twenty-eight people in 1968. He was convicted in 1971. He did not arrive in prison until 1974 and was out before the end of the year. So much for military justice. He killed twenty-eight people and served less prison time than I. I guess yellow people had about as little value as blacks.

Chuck Colson, founder and Chairman of Prison Fellowship Ministries, agrees with me that Fort Leavenworth is one of the most ominous-looking prisons in the country today. Its outside walls consist of huge stones stacked upon one another. Guard towers are spaced evenly around this formidable-looking barrier. Upon entering through its gates, one is struck by the view of the main building affectionately called the Castle. The Castle is made up of eight wings with a large control center in the middle causing it to look like some kind of petrified, monstrous octopus.

About twenty of us convict fish were unloaded at the gate of the facility and marched past the other buildings on the prison grounds. As we walked side by side, the other inmates, also men, made catcalls to us from the windows of the buildings. This was as unnerving an event as I have ever encountered. We had been warned before we got there that homosexual rapes were not uncommon there. After a brief initial orientation meeting with the assistant commandant, Colonel Buffalo, we were assigned to temporary cells in the section of the prison that served as death row when the army practiced capital punishment. After a week of orientation, we were assigned to more permanent cells in the general population. We had been properly welcomed to the United States Disciplinary Barracks.

I was placed on the top tier of seven wing. Cells in this prison are stacked about eight levels high. In the searing, dry heat of the summer, being in a cell close to the top was like cooking in an oven. The cells are only big enough for a man to lie down in, about 4' by

8' and made totally of steel and concrete. The sinks in the cells are made so that the water merely trickles down the side of the bowl, making it impossible for a person to cup their hands under the faucet to get a drink of the warm water that ran from it. It is against the rules to have any type of cup in one's cell. At night the dry Kansas air was stifling. Men screamed all kinds of obscenities all night long. As I lay there cooking in my own personal oven, unable to moisten my dry tongue with a simple drink of water, I could imagine what hell must be like. Like few others, I can to a degree relate to the feelings of the rich man who went to hell and was so tormented by the heat of the flames he asked Father Abraham to allow Lazarus to be sent to him to provide him with a drop of water to cool his tongue.

It was while lying on my bunk in that cell that I began to seriously contemplate anew the concept of God in any deep manner since I had been grown. As a child, I had committed my life to Christ. As a young man, I embraced Islam, albeit ever so halfheartedly. For the past several years, if ever asked about my feelings on religion, I claimed to be an agnostic. Now I had a lot of time to think about God. Through these many hours of contemplation, I came to the conclusion that God definitely is real. His creation was too perfect. His greatest creation, man, was too intricately made to have been a cosmic happenstance. Yes, God exists, I admitted to myself, but who is He? Is He the God of the Christians or the Muslims?

I understand that prisons are needed to protect society from its most dangerous criminals. Prison, however, is one of the greatest failures of our society. The proof of this is that most prisoners will return once released. The institution itself has no real power to change anyone for the better. The best benefit that prison can provide is to give a person time to think. Most prisoners will give more thought to spiritual issues in prison than at any other point in their lives. Now, forcibly taken off the treadmill of addiction and street life, I was able to think clearly for the first time in years. My thoughts turned to God.

While in prison, I did not attend any religious services. I

respected the Muslims and the Christians, the two main faiths in the prison. I would not make a commitment to either. There were no outside churches or Christian organizations ministering in that prison while I was there that I knew of. Chuck Colson, at that time, was himself serving time in a federal prison in another state for a Watergate-related offense. Prison Fellowship would not be started for yet another year.

Fort Leavenworth housed all levels of prisoners. At one point it even housed prisoners sentenced to death. There were men serving as long as fifty- and sixty-year sentences. There were men like myself serving short sentences. Many of the men serving twenty-year or longer sentences, considered life sentences, were Vietnam veterans. Most of these men had killed their officers either by intentionally shooting them in combat situations or by "fragging" them. The term "fragging" referred to the practice of throwing a live hand grenade into a man's tent. Their aim was for the fragments of shrapnel to kill the person. Prisoners there represented three branches of the armed forces, the army, the air force and the marines.

There were also quite a number of guys there who had served in West Germany. Many of them I knew from the White Horse. A few of them I knew from Schwäbisch Gmünd. One of the men I had known from the White Horse who came to Fort Leavenworth after me told me that Bosley had died from a hotshot. A hotshot is a pack of rat poison (strychnine) packaged to look like heroin. The unsuspecting person shoots it into his vein believing it to be heroin, only to die like a rat. I wondered whether the Frenchman had finally caught up to Bosley or whether he had simply crossed one person too many. I felt no emotion hearing of his death. Also, I learned that Skip was the snitch that Captain Jacobson had warned me about. Skip had gotten caught boosting from a store in town. The MPs threatened to send him to prison if he did not tell who was selling drugs on the post. He sang like a bird, informing on me and every other drug dealer he knew of to save his own worthless hide.

Having only a one-year sentence made me a short-timer coming in the door. I was determined not to get into any trouble that would prolong my stay in this hellhole. My good conduct was rewarded by my being transferred to the honor wing after about two months in the general population. In the honor wing inmates had a few more privileges than those in the general population. The honor wing was also made up of two-person cells that were a lot more spacious. What should have been a welcome relief to me turned out to be two months of horror.

Only I could have been lucky enough to be placed in a cell with one of the most notorious convicts in the prison. There was a man who had arrived at Fort Leavenworth shortly before I got there. This man had shot four of his good friends, killing three of them. The story was well published around the institution. They were stationed in Germany. My new cellmate, Harrison, was the kind of person that the guys liked to kid a lot, play practical jokes on. One evening they had been in his room smoking hashish and drinking. He had earlier taken a psychedelic drug. They got the munchies and began to rummage through the small refrigerator that he and his roommate shared. They began to eat some bologna that belonged to his roommate. He asked them several times not to eat the bologna, fearing his roommate would be angry. They ignored and laughed at him. Because of their ridicule he was driven to tears.

Harrison, humiliated, left the room in tears going to where he knew a fellow soldier was walking guard duty with live ammunition. He convinced this man that the Officer of the Day needed to see him and that he had been sent to relieve him from guard duty. Stupidly, this soldier handed his loaded gun to my cellmate. Harrison climbed into the window of his room where the four men were still hanging out and sprayed the room with the M-16.

I was horror-stricken having been placed in the cell with this man. Surely he was mentally unstable. What if he had a flashback? I was truly caught between a rock and a hard place. I reasoned that I could not go to the head guard to ask for a transfer to another cell, for the guard was likely to investigate my request for a change by asking Harrison if there had been any trouble between us. In all actuality, there had been no trouble between us. It would be a good chance that my request for a change would be denied, and I would be left locked in the cell with a now angry, crazy person. I, instead, pretended to be his friend, acting as if his horrific act did not bother me. I would simply have to ride this one out. If I perished, I perished.

Once, after we had come back to our cell after work, we both fell asleep while waiting for count and chow call. The way the system worked was that when inmates were informed over the speaker system that it was time for their respective wing to go to the chow hall, the cell doors were momentarily unlocked. The inmate had to stand by his door, opening it before it was locked back. If you did not open your cell door during this brief moment, it was automatically re-locked.

My cellmate and I woke up about ten minutes after everyone else had gone to chow. We discovered that the door was locked. We stood there calling for the guard to let us out so we could go to chow. We called and called; yet no one responded. Then he turned to me with a very strange expression on his face and dryly commented, "Man, you could be killing somebody in here and the guards would not even come."

"Guaaaarrrrrrd!" I yelled as loud as I could this time. I didn't know just how serious he was. I didn't want to find out, either.

Instantly, I became the object of pity of all the other inmates. They talked to me as if I had a terminal illness. "Do you know what your cellmate was sent to prison for?" they would ask. "Yeah, I know," I would sadly reply. Most of the time they just stared at me, not knowing what to say. If he had killed his friends over a pack of bologna, it wouldn't take much for him to do me in. My cellmate, although quite obviously mentally ill, never tried to kill me. I certainly tried hard not to give him any cause. After two months I was moved to a lower custody level. My living horror was over.

Every inmate at Fort Leavenworth had the opportunity to learn a trade. I chose the trade of furniture upholstery. I chose this trade not because I planned to work at it when I got out but because I wanted to make a chess set out of whiskey barrels. I was told that I had to work in the upholstery shop in order to engage in that kind of project. After being assigned to the upholstery shop, I learned that I really had a knack for this type of work. I had never before realized that I could do something so constructive with my hands. I enjoyed working in the upholstery shop. We upholstered the furniture of military personnel and civilians who worked for the army in and near the fort. That and taking a couple of college courses made my time go by swiftly. Little did I know it then, but God would later use this very trade to literally save my life and to restore my relationship with Him.

My out date was set for April 19, 1975. I was excited at the prospect of going back home after being away for nearly three years. I had serious concerns, though, whether I would really make it all the way home. There may be a sheriff's deputy waiting for me to step off the airplane at Detroit's Metro Airport. This was the experience of many of the men who had, like me, fled into the army in an attempt to avoid prosecution in their home state. I didn't tell anyone of the case I had run away from back in Detroit, fearing someone might snitch on me for some kind of brownie points.

Having totally forgotten the promise I had made to God back in the German prison, I had every intention of resuming my criminal career upon release. We had a saying when someone asked us if we were going to go straight when we got out of prison. "Yeah, I am going straight to the dope-house when I get out," we would respond.

10

BACK TO
THE WORLD

B ack to the world" was an expression that started in Vietnam by
black GIs. Nam had been such a stark contrast to the lives they
had lived in the ghettos, small towns, and rural areas back in the
States. So different was the exotic, violent world of Vietnam that it
seemed to them as if it were on another planet or dimension, one
that had no real connection to the neighborhoods and rural areas
from which they had come. So when they fantasized about returning home, they referred to it as going back to the world. As Vietnam
veterans were rotated from the war zone and stationed in posts
throughout the world, they introduced other soldiers to certain
aspects of the culture of the Vietnam War, such as dap and the
expression "back to the world." It was my turn now to go back to
the world. I had no idea what kind of world I would be returning
to.

There were no deputies awaiting my arrival at the airport. It
seems that my coming back to town had gone as undetected as my
leaving had been. I was safe for now. I learned that much had
changed since I had been gone. Mamma and Dad were still the
same old folks, although in their old age they were learning to get
along without physical violence. Dad had developed a crippling
form of arthritis in his legs that caused him to retire early from

Ford. He was not able to get around nearly as well as before. Mamma probably could have whipped him now had she wanted to. But she didn't. Mike was in state prison at the time serving his second sentence for armed robbery. He had only stayed out of prison after his first prison term for about four months before being re-arrested. We found out that he had gotten into a fight with one of the guards in Jackson Prison and been beaten nearly to death by the "goon squad." The goon squad was comprised of the biggest, meanest prison guards in a facility. They were specially trained to subdue unruly inmates using special shields, mustard gas, mattresses, and other implements. After the beating, he began to experience frequent grand mal seizures. Physically and mentally, he would never be the same. Harold was out of the army now, living with Dedee, not far from where she and I had lived before I went into the Army. He was using his GI Bill to attend electronics classes. Dedee worked at a Church's Chicken restaurant to raise her son. Bam had worked for Chevrolet for a number of years since being released from prison. Although maintaining a job, he usually pursued some kind of illegal activity to supplement his income. I learned that he had just shut down a fairly successful gambling operation and was now a partner in another after-hours gambling establishment.

I connected with my old friends the same day I returned home. On one occasion shortly after returning home, Vincent King and I stood outside his house in the old neighborhood. At the time we were contemplating how to get some money so we could get high. We observed a group of older ladies coming up the street toward us. I recognized one of the ladies as the mother of a friend of ours, Stevie West. Mrs. West was known to be a Spirit-filled Christian. As they proceeded toward us they stopped, praying for everyone they met along the way. Finally they arrived to where we were standing. "Can we pray for you boys?" Mrs. West asked. "Yes ma'am, go ahead," we both agreed. It couldn't hurt, I reasoned. Maybe their prayers would be good luck and I would hit the number.

The ladies surrounded us, placing their hands on our backs and on our shoulders. They began to pray. "Oh Lord," one of them began, "don't let these young men have no success until they decide to turn their lives over to You and serve You," they prayed. "Yes Lord, yes Lord," they all agreed. Then they walked away. Vincent and I were stunned. We both believed in the power of prayer. How could they have prayed such a prayer on us? Instead of blessing us, it seemed as if they had heaped the ultimate curse upon us. The words of this prayer would haunt me until I indeed decided to turn my life over to Him. I believe God honored the words of these mighty prayer warriors as Vincent and I many years later sat in church together, the only two from our circle that managed to escape the chaotic world in which we were entangled. As we sat in my living room with my children swirling about us, we laughed as we recounted that experience. *Mrs. West, God bless you and your group for that wonderful prayer!*

I moved in with Bam after staying with Dedee and Harold for a short period. They did not have enough room for me to stay there, nor did they possess the criminal mind-set that Bam and I shared. "After-hour joints," as we called them, were popular places for local criminals to hang out. Being the proprietor of one of these establishments brought Bam into contact with people from all of the street trades. Bam had always been a very congenial person. He made friends with a number of high-level drug dealers at his club.

Bam's partner was a man by the name of Lonnell. Lonnell was a hustler from the old days. Nearly two decades older than Bam, he had made his living in the streets for as long as anyone could remember. Consequently, he had served a couple of prison terms, which is looked upon by criminals, in that day anyway, as a hazard that comes with the job. Actually, my having spent time in prison, albeit a relatively short sentence, provided me with a new status in the criminal world. I was now part of what was then a select fraternity.

While serving a term at the federal prison in Leavenworth, which is a stone's throw from the institution in which I served my time, Lonnell met a man who was a member of the Mafia by the name of Joe Caracci. The two men became good friends. Both being from Detroit, they continued their association once released.

Joe, who was an old man when I knew him, was now the Mafia

boss for all of southeastern Michigan. He had a private club in downtown Detroit that he had used in the past as a gambling house for high rollers. Since he was not currently using this facility, he allowed Lonnell and Bam to use it as their own after-hours joint. I hung around this joint quite a bit, as I sought to find a niche once again in the Detroit crime world. Joe really took a liking to me; first, because we shared the same first name; second, because we had served time in institutions that were in close proximity to each other.

Realizing that I would not be able to immediately get back in to the swing of things, criminally speaking, I found a job upholstering furniture in the daytime. At night I worked hard at connecting with the new movers and shakers in the criminal world. Before I went into the army, Bam had not been interested in the drug trade. Now, however, after observing many of his friends make hundreds of thousands of dollars in this lucrative business, he began to develop an appetite for the fast money that only drug dealing could provide.

Bam and I stopped by Sister's house for a visit one evening. Kenny had a ten-speed bike that he agreed to loan to me so that I could get around town since I did not have a car. We loaded the bike into the backseat of Bam's gold 1974 Monte Carlo. I asked Bam to stop by the store to get some snacks before going home. Bam decided to take me to a store in Dearborn, a nearby suburb of Detroit. As we pulled out from the parking lot of the store, blue lights began to flash at our rear. It was the Dearborn police. Dearborn, the hometown of Henry Ford, was an exclusively white city that had an extensive history of racial segregation. Blacks could go there in the daytime to work. At night the police often harassed any blacks they saw passing through their city. Obviously, they wanted to check out whether we two black men had stolen a bike from some poor suburban child.

I handed the officer who approached the passenger side of the car a piece of identification. The two officers sat in their car as Bam and I sat in the Monte Carlo. The officer's car radio was loud enough for me to hear the dispatcher tell them that I had an outstanding warrant. I was out of prison for a little over a month and was headed back to jail. I would beat Mike's record of four months.

Sitting in the holding cell behind the courtroom in Frank Murphy Hall of Justice, I wondered how much time I would get this time. It was not a matter of whether I could avoid going to prison. It was a certainty, I thought. This time I even had a prison record. I would probably receive a longer sentence than I would have had I not skipped out in the first place.

Someone was walking up the hallway outside the holding cells calling my name. I had no idea who it was. "I'm down here," I called out. I was shocked to learn that it was Herman, my old lawyer. "Where have you been for these three years?" Herman quizzed me. "I have been looking for you so that we could go to court and get this thing taken care of," he scolded me. Herman had been going through the courtroom dockets of judges who were friendly to him. I was told that his legal strategy was to try to only work with judges who were his friends. If a client of his was scheduled to appear before a judge with whom he did not have this kind of relationship, he motioned to have the case moved before a friendly judge. This way he could count on their leniency. He no doubt slipped them a few bucks on the side. While searching the dockets, he came across my name. Amazingly, he remembered my name and my case. Ashamed that I had skipped out of town owing Herman money, I slowly replied, "I've been in the army."

"Great," Herman exclaimed without questioning me further. He wrongly assumed that I had not gotten into any trouble in the army. Quickly, he ducked back into the courtroom. In a few minutes he was back in front of the bars. "Will you accept two years' probation?" he anxiously asked. "Probation!" I shouted. "Yeah, I'll take it if I can get it."

Once again I stood before the bar of justice, my fate in the hands of another man. "Mr. Williams, I see that you were arrested last night on an outstanding warrant. Please tell the court why you failed to appear in August of 1972." Judge Jiles ordered.

It quickly became apparent that the Detroit authorities did not have access to my military and prison records. Surely, whatever I said in court would be checked out, though. I hoped the judge would not question me about my military career. "Your honor," I began, "while I was waiting to go to court, I received my draft notice in the mail. For the last three years I have been in the army." I hoped against hope this would satisfy him.

"What happened after the three years, Mr. Williams?" Judge Jiles continued to question.

"I got out of the army last month," I replied.

Then he asked the question I had been dreading. "You received an honorable discharge and got out of the service?" he asked.

My heart was now in my throat. Without even thinking and with a straight, serious face I replied, "Yes sir."

"In light of your military service to this country, I am going to sentence you to two years' probation," the judge responded. My demeanor remained calm but on the inside my heart was shouting, "Yes! Yes!"

"Are you drug free, Mr. Williams?" the judge asked.

I really hoped that he would keep my drug use out of this. "Yes your honor, I'm drug free," I again lied. Hey, I was on a roll.

I was taken down to the probation office to have a urine test administered that would determine whether I was truly drug free. Should I test negative, the conditions of my parole would not require me to report. Fortunately for me, I had not been able to get any drugs to use for the past three days. Heroin only remains in a person's urine for three days. This was one of the rare times in the past seven years that my urine was clean, barring prison.

Herman shook my hand and assured me that he still wanted his fee. I likewise assured him that he would certainly receive it. Thanking Herman profusely, I walked out of the court building for the first time in three years not having to worry about this case. A free man! I was free on the outside, that is. The criminal lifestyle I had bought into and my addiction had me bound tighter than any prison could have ever held me. It would be years still before I found true freedom.

Bam and I reasoned that between us we possessed a good combination. I had experience in selling drugs. He now had connections with major drug dealers who could supply us with quality products to sell. We decided to make a go of it. The Williams brothers were in business. We tried unsuccessfully to talk Harold into joining the police force so that we could have a man on the inside. He wisely would have no part in it.

We tried dealing heroin in a number of locations without much success. Since I had been away, I naturally had lost most of my clientele. I still had a few faithful people who were willing to patronize me—mostly longtime friends and acquaintances. For years we tried unsuccessfully to establish a thriving drug business. There were periods when I attempted to get something going on my own and with other partners. I only experienced short-term limited success. Bam experienced similar frustrations. While operating a drug house on Burnette Street on the far west side, Bam was raided by the narcotics squad. At that time, he worked the house in the daytime while I worked at a large retail furniture and upholstery company. I worked the house at night and slept there. Like I had been, he was charged with violation of the state narcotics law. Also, like me, he failed to appear in court and became a man on the run.

In the summer of 1977, Bam lived in a rented house a couple of streets from the house on Burnette where he had been raided about six months earlier. This house on Rangoon Street was uniquely located on a dead-end street where he had only two other neighbors. He lived there with his common-law wife Della and their two children, Onika, who was about three years old, and Romana, who was an infant. Bam had a teenage daughter, Nettie, who didn't live with him, but lived with her mother on the north end.

Bam and Lonnell had established a connection with one of the largest drug dealers in Detroit. This man dealt directly with the Mafia. This provided Bam with a steady supply of high-grade heroin. He began selling heroin from the house on Rangoon and recruited me to work for him. A new form of heroin had now become very popular in Detroit around this time, which we called "mixed jive." Mixed jive was a combination of a small amount of heroin mixed with other chemicals such as quinine, lactose, and a sleeping medication called Dormine. Mixed jive was cheaper to use than so-called "pure jive." Properly preparing this mixture became a valuable skill. Bam learned to mix the drugs, then taught me the recipe and the method.

By this time, because of constant shortage of funds, I had begun to use mixed jive as well. Part of my compensation package from Bam was an allotted amount of drugs each day. Unsatisfied with the effects of the unmixed drugs, I began to use my drug allowance to make my own personal stash of mixed jive. This cheap street mixture was known to cause severe medical problems after prolonged or excessive use. Because I had a nearly inexhaustible supply of drugs, I soon began to suffer ill effects.

Missing the vein when injecting mixed jive meant certain extreme swelling of the area of the body into which the drug was injected. As my veins became harder, narrower, and more difficult to find and hit, I experienced a lot of misses. Soon my arms were swollen grotesquely. My hands grew to the size of small boxing gloves. Even worse, I began to develop abscesses or skin ulcers.

These ill effects did not slow my use of the drug. Rather, not having had access to this quantity of drugs since I had been in Germany, I hoggishly pursued this coveted high.

After the drug operation on Rangoon became successful, Bam moved himself and his family to another house. He left me with a crew to run the operation on my own. My hands and arms were swollen and fluid-filled. They were about twice their normal size. One morning as I was washing up in the sink, I held my tender hands under the warm water. Suddenly, the poison in my arms and hands found the weakest point in my skin, which was on my wrist. The water, which had been clear, quickly turned pale red as a seemingly endless stream of fluid broke through the abscess on my wrist into the bowl of the sink.

I knew that I would no longer be able to avoid going to the doctor for treatment. The nurse at the clinic noticed blue streaks running the length of both of my arms. He feared that I had contracted gangrene and would have to have both arms amputated. After a brief examination, I was referred to Detroit General Hospital, which was known as Receiving Hospital, for immediate admittance. The doctors at Receiving informed me that I had a massive infection in both hands, arms, and feet. All these areas were covered with open abscesses. It was discovered that osteomyelitis (bone infection) had set into the knuckle of the ring finger on my right hand. That knuckle was totally eaten away by the infection. The flesh was literally rotting from my bones. To stop the infection, the hospital staff administered to me massive doses of antibiotics.

Once again in my distress I cried out to the Lord. Being back home with Mamma and other Christian relatives, I had pretty much settled in my heart that the God of the Bible, the God of my mother, of my youth, was the only God. I knew that if I was ever to get my life on track it would likely mean returning to the God of my mother—the God of my youth. Lying in the bed bandaged like a mummy, I began to read a Bible that was given to me by the hospital chaplain. Although I read it daily, I had little understanding of it. The doctors debated over whether to amputate my finger. I became very despondent just thinking about losing a part of my body, even though it was only a finger. The priests and the nuns did a wonderful job of ministering to me, lifting my spirits greatly. I shall never forget their kindness. They planted a seed in my heart. As bad off as I was, though, I knew I did not have the power to resist using drugs.

I spent about three weeks in the hospital. Business on Rangoon suffered greatly while I was in the hospital. Bam must have been extremely happy to see me back in the saddle. The crew Bam had left me with had totally deserted their post. It was up to me to put together a new crew. A man who was a longtime friend of our family whom we called Jukie had faithfully visited me in the hospital. Jukie had quite a bit of experience selling heroin and was looking for some work. We agreed that he should join my crew.

As it turned out, Jukie and I became a good team together. Jukie had a short temper and an itchy trigger finger. I reasoned that he was just the kind of person I needed to watch my back. While drug houses were frequently robbed, no one ever attempted to rob us because our security system was so tight. I was always a systematic person. I periodically drilled my team in regard to how they should respond in certain situations, such as attempted robberies and police raids. I used my raw administrative skills to build a drug operation that ran like the proverbial well-oiled machine.

Soon money began rolling in like the tide. Bam had other drug houses, but mine was his chief moneymaker. For the most part, we sold mixed jive for $12 per pack. As a sideline, we sold other drugs and ran a fencing operation. I paid Bam $9 for each pack I received. I gave Jukie $1 and kept $2 for myself. We sold hundreds of packs per day. I was making thousands. Bam was making tens of thousands.

Finally, I was experiencing the kind of success I had coveted for years. There was always plenty of action at the house on Rangoon. It seemed as if the world beat a path to my door. I did not have to go out to purchase anything. Electronic appliances, clothes, furs, furniture—all made their way to my door. I wore my hair in the popular style for players in that day, a Superfly. This hairdo, which involved growing one's hair long, chemically straightening it, then having it slightly curled or waved, was made popular by the movie of the same name. In that movie the main character was a drug dealer in Harlem, New York. His plan was to make a lot of money, then get out of the drug game. Although the character's name was Priest, everyone simply referred to him as Superfly. I identified with Superfly because my plan was the same as his. Superfly, however, was not a junkie like I was. I should have more readily identified with the character Freddy who was a low-level junkie drug dealer. When the stuff hit the fan, Freddy was the first to be killed. As Curtis Mayfield soulfully moaned in the movie soundtrack, *Freddy's dead, that's what I said. Another junkie's plan, pushin' dope for the Man—a terrible blow, but that's how it goes.* Would I end up like Freddy or Superfly? I wondered.

My bankroll was fat. My wardrobe was expansive. My signature outfit was a charcoal gray four-button suit with pinstripes. With it I wore a red long-collared shirt and wide, gray tie. I also wore red driving gloves that helped to cover the scars on my hands and red patent leather and suede shoes that had a glass heel with an ace of spades in the heel. You couldn't tell me I wasn't clean when I stepped out with that outfit on.

I was different, though, from most drug dealers in that I refused to sell hard drugs to teenagers. Many dealers engage in this practice in order to keep a steady stream of new customers. However, whenever a couple of the neighborhood teenagers came to my door thinking they were ready for graduation to hard drugs, I refused to sell to them. They were astonished as I, a drug dealer, admonished them to avoid using hard drugs at all cost. "Stick to the weed, kid," I would encourage them. "You don't need the misery that comes along with jive." These were not the words of a true wolf, but a sheep in disguise.

Once one of my regular customers, a young woman named Jackie, who was deeply addicted to heroin, said something to me that took me aback. She was proud of her veteran status as a street hustler and considered herself somewhat of a sage. She was a shapely, dark-skinned woman with a short-cropped, curly Afro. She was always neat and clean. I could tell that had her life taken a different turn she would have been a very attractive lady. The lines and scars on her ashen face, though, told a tale of many hard times and painful experiences. I did not know exactly what she did to make a living and to support her substantial drug habit. I assumed that she was involved in prostitution. Many women, though, who sold their bodies were also involved in other extracurricular activities. Women drug addicts often had to engage in shameful acts in order to stay supplied with drugs. I never heard much about what this particular woman was into. She never offered this kind of information on her own. I had what might be considered a "don't ask, don't tell" policy.

"Joe man, what are you doin' out here in all this madness?" she questioned. "What chu talkin' 'bout, girl?" I retorted.

"You ain't like the rest of us dopefiends out here. I mean, the rest of us out here don't have nothin' goin' for us. Ain't no way we can make it in the square world. You different, though. You could be doin' somethin' else. You could be doin' somethin' good," she so eloquently explained. I muttered some lame response along the lines of feeling that I was just as trapped as all the others who found themselves entangled in this crazy world. She took the drugs she had come to purchase, shook her head, and left.

The truth was that I felt just as trapped as Jackie and the others. She apparently saw something in me that I did not recognize in myself. She saw a glimpse of the *sheep* in me that I was desperately attempting to suppress. I knew I had some intelligence and skills that would allow me to flourish in the real world. My deep love for heroin, though, would never allow me to escape this horrible pit, I thought.

Many nights after we closed down the operation, we went to Lonnell's after-hours joint on Chene and Garfield over on the east side. For a while, as sole proprietor, Lonnell operated a popular joint called the Purple Door. Virtually every player in the city knew Lonnell and patronized his joint. I thoroughly enjoyed hanging out at John's with the other players. Lonnel always allowed me to keep my pistol while making others either leave theirs in their car or check them at the door. He wanted his close friends to remain armed so that we could have his back in the event anything broke out.

After experiencing a great deal of success with the Purple Door, Lonnell purchased a larger building across the street and became partners with a local businessman by the name of Mr. Coley. Mr. Coley owned a popular legitimate nightclub just down the street on Chene. They decorated it very elegantly, as far as after-hours joints go. This joint, which they named the 19th Hole, became the most popular after-hours joint in the city. People from all over attempted to gain entry into this exclusive club. Many were turned down at the door. I was a regular.

Everything was going well for me. I had all the money I could spend. I was able to give expensive presents to my family members. I wore expensive clothes, drove a nice car, and lived in a nice place. All the women loved me, they said. Why then did I attempt to take my own life?

Perhaps the saddest day of my life occurred when I realized that while I had attained everything for which I had striven for years, my life was as empty as ever. Not only was my life empty, but I was a slave to drugs. The absurdity of my being enslaved by a simple white powder was more than I could bear. Many times since I had been home from prison I tried to stop using the drug. Each time failure dogged my heels. I had heard somewhere that you are all you would ever be by the age of twenty-five. I was now twenty-five years old and was a drug-addicted criminal. If this was all there was and ever would be of my life, I would save myself the continued pain by ending it now.

One evening as Jukie handled the business of the house, I told him that I was tired and was going to bed. I had acquired about fifteen #10 Valiums and a bottle of cognac. I loaded my cooker with four times my normal dose of heroin. Taking the needle out of my arm, I dumped the pills into my oversized palm. Washing down the pills with a mouthful of cognac, I settled back into the bed for what I hoped would be my eternal rest. Yes, I had guns that would have done the job a lot quicker, but I would die as I had lived for so long. This way would be less painful as well, I reasoned. I continued to swill down the cognac as long as I was conscious.

It was beyond my comprehension that I woke up the next morning alive and feeling quite rested. I had taken enough drugs and alcohol into my body to kill two dopefiends; yet I was very much alive. Weeping uncontrollably, I sank to the floor. Why could I not even commit suicide right? After about a half an hour of contemplation I reasoned that I had not died because God had decided that it was not my time. Apparently, He had something for me to do. But how could I do anything for God in this condition?

Bam sensed that I was sliding into deep depression. He did not know how to communicate with me on this level, so he got a good friend of his by the name of Sweet Bee to counsel me. Bee was a bisexual in transition to becoming a lesbian. She was about as tough as any man I knew. She had been a large-scale drug dealer for many years and was well respected in the criminal community. We sat on my bed and talked. I explained to Bee that because my hands now bore the unmistakable scars of a dopefiend, I was trapped permanently in this world of chaos and danger. I could not move any further up the ladder as a drug dealer. No major drug dealer would ever trust an IV drug user. They felt the police and others too easily manipulated us. Nor could I ever expect to be accepted in or move unnoticed in legitimate society ever again.

"Everybody's got problems, Joe," she counseled. "You'd be surprised at the problems some   have," she continued. "The only difference between you and them is that your problem shows on the outside. A lot of them are able to hide theirs because it's on the inside," she counseled. We sat there talking for about an hour. Her words were comforting and seemed sensible. I will always appreciate the time Bee took to console me that evening. Our talk made me feel a lot better. I was able to continue for another day. Bee, I am afraid, missed her calling as a psychologist.

Bam and I began to have strong disagreements concerning my compensation. I was making a great deal of money for him. He was getting rich while I was settling for peanuts, it seemed. Additionally, I was taking all the chances. When the police came, I would be the one hauled away to jail and possibly prison. Bam did not agree that I should receive a raise. Negotiation was not a skill that was practiced and taught in our family. I was certain that I was not receiving fair treatment. Bam was sure that I did not have a raise in pay coming. We were at an impasse. Neither of us knew how much we needed each other. Our relationship began to suffer.

Bam had begun to use the drug he sold like so many other dealers. He was becoming entangled in a web from which it would take him many years to become free. Della had used heroin for years. Between the two of them they consumed a massive amount of drugs. Now, a drug dealer who begins to use his own product will not be in business for long. A drug dealer who also has a woman who uses drugs places himself in double jeopardy. As a result of drug use and unrestrained spending, the tens of thousands Bam had accumulated began to dwindle.

The relationship between Bam and me became quite strained. Feeling cheated, I lost all enthusiasm to continue to work for Bam. As a result, the business began to suffer. Jukie was caught driving my car by the police, which was a stolen car. One of my customers was a car thief who would change the VIN number on the dashboard so the police would not recognize it as stolen unless they really checked it out. This same customer became angry with me because of an unrelated transaction and decided to inform the police that I drove a stolen car. Jukie had taken the car earlier in the day. He was supposed to have brought the car back after only a couple of hours. Instead he kept it much longer. When he pulled up to the house, the police were waiting for him. He was arrested and sentenced to three to five years in Jackson Prison. Had Jukie brought the car back when he was supposed to, it would have been me arrested that day instead of him. On top of that, I probably would have been caught with drugs and a handgun.

Eventually, the house on Rangoon Street became unproductive. Bam and I came to a parting of the ways. We would never work together again. We each tried unsuccessfully to separately become reestablished in the drug business on several occasions. With the house on Rangoon closed down, we each suffered a great deal of difficulty trying to survive. We each had dealer's habits. We each had become accustomed to living well. Times became quite desperate for both of us. Our desperation drove us to resort to drastic measures on a number of occasions.

During the time we ran the aforementioned drug operation, Mike was released from prison. The beating he had received from the prison guards disabled him both physically and mentally. Physically he was uncoordinated, while mentally his thought processes were a beat slow. He suffered frequent violent seizures. Since he was not able to take care of himself, I did what I could to help him when my income was good and steady. As an unemployed drug dealer, this would prove quite a difficult task.

//
DOPEFIEND DADDY

By 1979 the country was in the throes of a devastating recession. We were actually experiencing a depression in Detroit. Someone once said that when white America has a cold, the black community will have pneumonia. Detroit, being a chocolate city, was lying at death's door. So many people were fleeing the city that a prominent television newscaster asked that the last one out of the city turn out the lights. The lights are still burning, however, and he is no longer around.

Men and women were laid off from the auto factories in droves. Entire factories closed down. Many people do not realize that when the working citizens of a community begin to suffer economically, the criminals suffer twice over. Most of the players I knew were catching about as much grief as I was—and I was catching it.

After the working relationship between Bam and I deteriorated, I began to drive a taxi while remaining constantly on the lookout for illegal opportunities. Cab driving provided me with an income as well as a vehicle in which to get around. I secured an efficiency apartment on Broadstreet only a few blocks from where my parents lived. Mike lived with me. Ron Fisher from the old neighborhood also lived with me most of the time. Bam dropped in for a multi-day respite from time to time. Sometimes there would be so many of us packed into the tiny apartment that Ron would be forced to sleep under the Murphy bed. By now Bam had begun to inject heroin. He was in worse shape than I was.

One day as we desperadoes sat in the apartment trying to figure out a way to make some illegal money, Bam called on the phone, informing me that a guy who had once sold drugs for me after my split with him was in business again. This man had concocted a scheme to cheat me out of my drugs. He made up some wild story about how he lost the drugs. At the time the money I made from him dealing for me was my only income. I could have easily killed him for that. Instead, I took everything of value in his house. As I left his front door hauling appliances, rugs, curtains, etc., I warned him that he still owed me, and that if I ever heard that he had some money, I was going to take it.

"Hey Joe," Bam uttered through the phone. "I just heard that that punk Jerry is selling jive. He's supposed to be doing pretty good from what I hear," he related.

Surely Jerry didn't think he could sell drugs without paying me what he owed me. My cupboards were bare. My clothes were wearing out. I was living from day to day. Now why should he be making all that money while I suffered?

"Ron, Bam just told me that Jerry is dealing jive. You wanna ride over there with me while I kick his   and take my money from him?" Ron was more than game for some action. We quickly slipped on our shoes and coats to leave. Ron had a long .38 Police Special and I had a 9 mm. We trotted down the stairs, got in Ron's ancient Black Fleetwood, and headed toward Jerry's. I asked Ron to watch my back while I took good care of the treacherous Jerry. Ron agreed that he would.

Jerry's eyes bucked wide when he realized that it was me at the door. He let me in wearing a fake nervous smile on his face. Ron walked in behind me. Jerry's common-law wife, Diane, was in the kitchen with their two young children.

"Hey, Jerry, I heard you got some jive for sale, man. I want some," I began. "Naw man, I'm out right now. I expect to have something in about an hour," he attempted to convince me. I didn't believe him. I didn't want to believe that I had the bad luck of catching him when he didn't have anything.

"There someplace we can talk in private?" I inquired. I didn't want to beat him down in front of his kids.

"We can talk in the bedroom," Jerry nervously offered.

When we got into the bedroom I pulled the 9 mm from under my coat. Jerry's eyes grew as large as saucers. "Nigga," I viciously growled, "didn't I tell you that whenever you got some money it was mine?" I shouted. Like lightening, my fist connected with the center of his face. Jerry fell backward, limply dropping to the ground. As he fell, the side of his head struck the corner of the dresser. He sat slumped in the corner with his eyes rolling around in his head.

I punched him several times as he lay on the floor. "Punk, I'm going to kill you right here if you don't stop lying to me and give me my money," I assured him. I was furious at this point. I would have never killed him in front of witnesses though. However, I wanted him to believe that I would so he would not hold out on me.

"Joe, I swear," Jerry sobbed. "I don't have the money. If I did I would give it to you, man. You know I would. Please don't kill me," he pleaded.

As I stood with my back facing the kitchen, working Jerry over, Diane slowly slipped her slender, caramel-colored hand into the kitchen drawer next to her, finally clutching a snub-nose .38. " , put the gun down," I heard Rod snarl in his best Humphrey Bogart imitation. I turned to see Diane holding her hands in the air as Ron held the gun with which she had hoped to blow out my back.

Looking back down at Jerry, he was now more frightened than ever. He was totally drenched in perspiration. Grabbing him in the collar of his sweat-soaked shirt, I informed Jerry that he was henceforth out of business. He was not to sell any drugs unless he first checked with me. He agreed. "They ain't got nothin', man. Let's split," I called to Ron. Ron and I backed out of the house, got into the old Cadillac, and drove off. All we had for all our trouble was a pistol. Since he had done such a superb job at watching my back,

Ron insisted I let him keep the shorter pistol. I took the long-barrelled .38.

As is the case with many small apartment buildings, there was a lot of interaction going on among the residents. It seemed that the entire building was filled with misfits. There were several drug-addicted ex-offenders including me, winos, sexual perverts, and runaways. I dated a young lady who lived upstairs from me for a short while by the name of Dianna. She was only about eighteeen years old at the time. She had run away from her home in Saginaw, Michigan, when she was only fifteen. I guess it is no mystery why we gravitated toward each other. Although she had been on her own for some time, she was quite naïve concerning the drug world.

Darren Berry, my upstairs neighbor, Bobbie Tucker, my down-stairs neighbor, Ron Fisher, and I had been successful in acquiring some heroin. By now my veins were very difficult to hit. The danger always existed that if I hit into a narrow vein that allowed me to draw blood back into the syringe but was too small to inject the blood and heroin into, the whole mixture would jell before I could find a vein stout enough to accept the drug. The others had been successful in injecting their drugs. I was in the bathroom with blood in my syringe desperately trying to get a hit.

There was a knock at the door. Darren came into the bathroom to inform me that Dianna was at the apartment door. Dianna had never seen me shooting dope. She had never been around people shooting dope. "Tell her to come back later," I told Darren. He left the bathroom as I frantically tried to find a spot to inject my drugs. In a moment he was back. "She won't go away, man. She say she really need to see you," Darren stated. I could hear Dianna continue to knock on the door as I complained to Darren about his inept-ness in getting rid of a teenage girl.

I went to the door still frantically trying not to waste the quick-ly jelling dope in my syringe. Opening the door with my right hand, I held my blood-dripping left arm behind the door. "What you want, Dianna? Didn't Darren tell you I'm busy?" I asked in an annoyed tone.

"You ain't too busy to talk to me," she insisted. "Let me in."

"You can't come in now; we taking care of business. Say what you want through the door," I coaxed.

"Alright, I'm pregnant," she blurted. "That's your business," I retorted. "What you want me to do about it?" I asked.

"It's your baby," she insisted. "I want you to take care of it."

"How in the hell do you expect a dopefiend like me to take care of a baby?" I responded.

"You ain't no dopefiend," she tried to convince herself.

As incredible as it seems, I stood there at the door trying to convince Dianna that I was indeed a dopefiend. Unsuccessful in convincing her verbally, exasperated, I flung the door open, exposing my left arm with the needle sticking in it now dripping blood to the floor. "You know what a dopefiend looks like now. You want a dopefiend for the daddy of your baby?" I shouted.

Stunned, Dianna stumbled backward, finally resting against the wall opposite my apartment door. "I don't give a damn what you do," I screamed at her. "Get an abortion. Then you won't have to worry about it," I counseled. "I ain't killin' my baby," she retorted. Dianna turned and ran out the door that led to the hallway. Crushed by my words and what she had witnessed, she promptly returned to Saginaw to have her baby. I wouldn't see her again until three weeks after she delivered our son.

I didn't know at that time how the scene at my apartment door had affected Dianna. Without a doubt, it haunted me to no end. I had done some sleazy things in my day, but I had never before sunk so low. Mike, once as notorious as they come, sharply rebuked me for my actions. "Nigga, you know that's your baby. You should be ashamed of yourself the way you treated that girl," Mike scolded me. His words and that scene played in my head over and over. Finally, I began to acknowledge my responsibility.

I tried unsuccessfully to locate Dianna so I could at least offer her moral support through her pregnancy. I wanted to let her know that I intended to attempt to be a father to our child. However, she was nowhere to be found. I feared I would never see her or my child again. Near the end of April 1980, I received a call from the Saginaw County Friend of the Court. The male social worker informed me that Dianna had named me as father of her son. I assured him that I intended to accept full responsibility. He was gracious enough to have her call me.

Dianna stayed with her sister, Rhoda, while she visited Detroit, providing me with the opportunity to get to know my son, Anthony. He was so small and beautiful. It was difficult to conceive that I could have been part of so great a miracle. One day as I went to visit Dianna and Anthony (I called him Tony), I stood over his crib watching his every move. Dianna had gone to a different part of the house to perform some task. Suddenly tears burst forth from my weary eyes. I began to sob uncontrollably. Standing there looking down upon his sweet face, I was given a revelation of what his life would be like having a drug addict for a father. He didn't stand a chance. I felt the pain he would experience growing up with no positive role model for a father. Surely, his life would be as pain-wracked and miserable as mine had been. "Oh my son, my son," I moaned. "I didn't do you any favor by bringing you here. I am not fit to be your father. You don't have a chance in this world, baby boy. I probably won't even be around to see you grow up. How could I have done it?" I wailed. I can't say how I knew these things. I just knew. Since then I have learned that children of ex-offenders are far more at risk of going to prison themselves than the general population. The children of substance abusers are far more likely to become substance abusers themselves. I had not read these things anywhere. No one had told me these things. I daresay that flesh and blood did not reveal this to me, but the Spirit of God.

Hearing the sobs, Dianna rushed into the room. She had heard my crying, but was not able to understand my words. "You are crying because you don't want him, ain't you?" she accused. "That ain't it," I insisted. This was not something I could explain to her. How could she understand? I didn't even understand.

This "responsibility" was such a new experience for me. Before, when I ate, my whole family ate. If I didn't eat, no one was hungry but me. If I screwed up, no one was hurt but me, or so I thought. Now I had responsibility for another human being. Also, I somehow knew that if I failed in my responsibility, I would have to answer to God. How did I know that? I can only say the Spirit revealed it to me.

I wanted to change my life now more than ever. This time it wasn't just for me but for Tony. I could not continue to live the way I lived and be a proper father for my son. Now I had an incentive to change. God had placed a hook into my heart. I could feel the rod of the Good Shepherd nudging me back toward the fold.

With the recession worsening, the cab business began to suffer greatly. People did not have money to spend on cab rides. They got around as best they could using alternative means. I could no longer depend on cab driving to make enough money to live. I had stopped attempting to do any upholstery work ever since my hands became so badly marred from the abscesses. I did not even believe my hands still possessed the agility to perform the sometimes intricate tasks required in upholstery. Looking through the want ads, I noticed several jobs for qualified upholsterers. I decided to give it a shot.

After calling several shops, I landed an interview at a shop in a nearby suburb. This shop paid by the piece. If a person could turn out the pieces at a fast pace, they could make a decent living. The shop owner hired me on the spot. Joyfully, I discovered that my hands, though still slightly swollen, were still able to do the work. I worked at that job for several months until I found work at a shop closer to home called NuWay Upholstering.

Now I had work, but I still had a drug habit. This habit would often make it difficult for me to go to work on a steady basis. Often when I was not able to acquire drugs, the sickness of withdrawal pains made it difficult for me to perform. When I attempted to work while suffering from withdrawal, my work was sloppy and unacceptable. Many of the men in my new shop drank hard liquor on a consistent basis. In the evening, after the shop was closed for business, someone would go to the liquor store to buy a fifth of whiskey. We sat around for hours drinking, laughing, and talking. These men used a legal drug. Because it was relatively cheap, they were able to get high just about every night and still function. Some even drank relatively small amounts during the day to calm their jitters. I reasoned that it would be better for me to drink instead of using heroin. At least then I could be more productive, or so I thought.

Actually, this is a strategy that is pursued by many drug addicts. They mix drug use with alcohol, which often leads to cross addiction. Alcohol and drugs are a deadly combination that often leads to an overdose. Some drug users totally switch to alcohol, a practice that is known as switching addictions. It never works. It is simply a matter of deciding which poison you wish to die from. It didn't work for me either.

The shop owner at NuWay, Stan, was notorious for not paying his employees on time. On payday he had more stories than *Reader's Digest*. Growing weary of not getting my money on Friday, often being strung along until the next payday, I was enticed to another shop about a mile away called Puckett Upholstering, where they were in need of an upholsterer. Henry Puckett, the owner/operator of the shop, was a nice guy who was a few years older than I was. He had left the auto factory to operate his own business. His plan was to turn what had once been a hobby for him into a lucrative business. Henry's wife Deborah thought this was a good idea for him because while he had been working in the factory his consumption of alcohol had steadily increased.

Henry was a strange type of alcoholic. He did not drink everyday; however, he could not hold his liquor. So whenever he did drink he was almost certain to pass out at some point. Some mornings Deborah would find Henry parked in the driveway, sprawled halfway out of his car, passed out. Lucky for him, his car knew its way home. There was a lot of drinking going on at Henry's shop, even during working hours. We even smoked weed in the back of the shop after business hours.

One summer day, Henry, his cousin Leo, who worked for him in an unskilled position, a friend of Henry's named Rob, and I were chilling in the back of the shop. I had smoked some weed about a half an hour earlier. We were engaged in our normal activity of drinking beer and talking stuff while listening to the radio. The radio was tuned to WJLB, a local R&B music station. As we talked, a song began to play that I had not heard before. I learned later that it was by a group by the name of The Winans. The name of the song was "The Question Is." The Winans are a contemporary gospel group whose music has a contemporary R&B beat, although its lyrics are distinctly Christian. This, their first hit song, was played on secular stations as well as gospel stations. As I began to listen to the words of this song, I quickly tuned out the trash talk of my peers and listened more intently to the song's lyrics. A couple of lines in the song really hit me hard. *The question is will I ever leave You? The question is will I do Your will? The question is when will Jesus return? Soon, soon, soon, soon!* These words hit me in the face like a sledgehammer.

I immediately sobered up as I contemplated these questions in my head. Yes, I had left the Lord. No, I was not doing His will. And if it was true that He was returning soon, then I was really in trouble, I reasoned. This song haunted me every time I heard it played.

The Winans, who are a group of brothers, were heavily criticized for their style of music. The older, more traditional leaders in the church felt that they should not have been making gospel music with a contemporary beat. According to those leaders, the Winans had sold out in order to gain popularity. I strongly disagree with this argument. I was not going to purposefully tune in to Christian music on my radio. I was not going to church. I believe that God used that song to help get my attention. I would not have heard this message if the Winans had not been brave enough to do that which was not popular—that which brought pressure upon them.

That argument still rages on in the church today. Artists like Kirk Franklin are still criticized for their contemporary style in Christian music. I am in favor of contemporary Christian music because it has the ability to reach young people who may not otherwise hear the gospel message. God used this music to help prepare my heart. I know He will use it to prepare the hearts of many others. Bless you, Winans!

God was getting my attention in some other ways as well that summer. Rob, who was not a Christian, frequently stopped by the shop to talk and get high. One day he handed me a piece of paper he said he wanted me to read. It was a gospel tract that someone on the street had given him. He thought the message of the tract had merit and wanted to pass it along to me. It was one of those scary tracts that depicted the end of the world. It contained illustrations of those who were ready when Jesus returned and those who were not. I knew I was not ready. I knew I was not living in a manner that was pleasing to God. I don't know that Rob ever became a Christian; yet God certainly used him to turn my attention to Him. The Winans' song and that tract would haunt me for months.

I had lost my apartment on Broadstreet because I had a problem paying my rent on time. Dianna had moved back to Detroit with Tony and was living in a slum apartment about 1/4 of a mile from my parents' home on Blaine Street, near Lindwood. Because I had no other place to go, she allowed me to move in with her, even though we had not been dating since her return to Detroit. We decided that we would try to be a family. I didn't know how I could pull this off with a substantial drug habit. I felt I had to keep trying, though.

By this time Jukie had gotten out of prison after serving nearly two years. He and Mike had begun to hang out together as they had before Mike had ever gone to prison. One day they stopped by the apartment to let me know that an old friend of ours by the name of Randy Turner was selling large quantities of heroin and was doing well. He wanted to talk to me about selling some drugs for him. I was tremendously excited to be getting another crack at the drug game. Work was slow at Puckett's, so my money stayed short. It was all Dianna and I could do to keep food on the table. This, I thought, was a great opportunity.

Jukie, Mike, and I went to visit Randy. Randy stayed only a few blocks from the apartment on Blaine. Randy truly was doing well. He lived in a brick two-family flat with his wife and two children. In his driveway was a pale yellow Cadillac Seville. He came to the door decked out in gold, diamonds, and a new pair of lizard shoes. Also in the house was a seedy-looking bunch of guys who had made a proposal to Randy to sell drugs on consignment for him. All of these men had been released from Jackson Prison within the year. They claimed to be part of a prison-rooted religion called Moorish Science. After observing them for only a short time, I realized they were merely a criminal gang masquerading as religious devotees. DaBey, the leader of this group, was a short, stout man whose demeanor demonstrated many years of street experience. His two followers who accompanied him on that occasion were Claude and Ramsey. They appeared to be totally directed by DaBey.

After a short meeting that included a small sample of the product Randy sold, it was established that we along with DaBey and his gang were to be a part of Randy's crew. Our mission was to expand his drug-dealing operation and, subsequently, his profits. We were desperate enough to try anything at this point. I felt that I did not have many more chances left. I was a desperado. I was willing to do whatever it took to survive, even to the point of taking a human life.

After leaving the meeting, Mike, Jukie, and I discussed our mutual distrust for DaBey and his boys. They seemed as if they had skullduggery on their minds. We agreed that we would take them out (kill them) if they got the least bit out of line.

My plan was to sell drugs from my apartment. I had to persuade Dianna to move back to Saginaw for a while as I used the apartment for a drug den. She, no doubt, was happy to go, since she was not used to the kind of lifestyle I lived and the kind of people with whom I ran. In addition, I had recently overdosed in the bathroom of the apartment. My old drug buddy Harry was in the bathroom with me helping me to get a hit. He brought me back around and laid me on the daybed in the living room. When I came to, Dianna had her suitcase in one hand and Tony in the other, heading out the door. This episode had frightened her tremendously. She thought I was dead or dying. She did not want to be the one to explain to my parents that their son had died a junkie's death in our shared apartment. I pleaded with her not to take Tony away, promising to get my act together—an empty promise I knew I could not fulfill.

Actually, that was the second time in two months I had overdosed. This was a strange experience for me, because even when I was in Germany shooting nearly pure dope, I had never before overdosed. The first time I "ODed" I can recall the moment prior to my coming back to consciousness. It was like I was in a very peaceful, cool place. I had never known such peace. I was drifting in a haze. Suddenly, I felt and saw hands from another dimension pulling me out of this peaceful haven. I resisted with all of my might. "No, no, no. I don't want to leave!" I cried out. Then I felt a rough hand slapping me across my face. A familiar voice called my name. It was my old crime and drug buddy, Donnie. I had ODed in his dope-house. He and another man were walking me up and down the street in an attempt to bring me back from the OD. When I realized what had happened, I resented Donnie's persistence in reviving me. I had finally reached dopefiend utopia, and he brought me back to my wretched existence.

After the second OD I began to feel that my life was coming to an end. It was as if death were on my trail. I did not expect to see the new year. Strangely enough, I did not fear death but looked upon it as an inevitability that I had avoided for a long time. I would have just as soon been dead as to continue to live the existence I was living. I even fantasized about my funeral. Would anyone cry? I imagined that my family would be somewhat relieved after all the discomfort I had caused them over the years. It was as if I were being drawn toward the grave just as I had felt drawn toward prison six years earlier—like a moth to a flame.

Randy reluctantly gave me a cash advance so that I could purchase a Greyhound bus ticket for Dianna and Tony and to pay a portion of the overdue rent on the apartment. Dianna and Tony moved to Saginaw with her mother. Once I got rolling with the drug operation, I was to acquire another apartment for us to live in. Then I would send for the two of them.

We three partners, Mike, Jukie, and I, now awaited our allotment of drugs to sell and guns with which to protect our operation. After about a week of being stalled by Randy, we grew impatient. We were not able to reach him on the phone. Whenever we went by his house his car would be in the driveway, but his wife always told us he was not home. We had no money, no drugs, and no food. What was up with Randy?

Finally Randy returned our phone calls. He was very abrasive over the phone. He told Jukie that he did not plan to give us anything—no drugs, no guns, no money, no nothing. It seems that Randy felt that Jukie and I had slighted him when we sold drugs on Rangoon Street. For a short period he had worked for us. We discontinued the relationship because he was always short with the money. He felt that on one particular occasion we made him feel less than a man. I could not recall the specific incident to which he referred. In any event, he did not plan to come through with his part of the verbal agreement we had made. His intentions through this whole scheme were to humiliate us. He failed in his attempt, though. He only succeeded in making us angrier and even more desperate. Now we had nothing. We had nothing to lose.

I had sent Tony and Dianna away and had no resources with which to bring them back. Mike moved into the apartment with me. Times were lean and mean. The rent quickly fell even more in the arrears. The utilities had been behind for some time. I received constant threats from the electric company. Summer was drawing to an end. Winter was quickly approaching. We had no idea how we would make it through the winter.

Things had also gotten very bad for Bam. Having lost his own apartment, he moved in with Mike and me. There were three of us living in that tiny apartment. Three desperate men! Since Bam and I operated on different schedules, we slept in the same bed in shifts. He took the day shift. The night shift was mine. Mike slept on the daybed in the living room. We had mice and roaches, but times were hard for them as well. We could not even spare a roach a crumb.

At this juncture I sat down and began to weigh my options. I could only come up with four: (1) I could go back to sticking up to acquire the money I so desperately needed; (2) I could get caught in the commission of a robbery and be sent back to prison—at least I would eat everyday and have a place to live and food to eat; (3) I could be killed in the act of committing a stickup; (4) or I could save everyone a lot of trouble and simply take my own life. Apparently God had made a mistake by short-circuiting my last suicide attempt.

12

THE GOOD
SHEPHERD

By the fall of 1981 the recession was kicking everybody's behind
in Detroit. It seemed as if everyone, young and old, was catching hell. Most of the players I knew were scrounging to some
degree. Many had become millionaires from the heroin trade,
entrapping others into a sticky web of addiction. Now, even heroin
sales were slow. Many addicts began to switch to alcohol and/or a
combination of pills we called T's and Blues. This combination produced a fake heroin high. Also, the quality of the heroin on the
streets was usually very poor.

The heroin epidemic had lasted for nearly fourteen years now,
having begun shortly after the 1967 civil uprising across the nation.
It had wrought a devastating impact on the black urban community. Once people slept in their backyards, or on their front porches.
Many never locked their doors, even at night, because of the respect
we had for each other's property. Now, residents were even afraid
to sleep in their locked houses, fearing that some junkie burglar
might break in and kill them. In many neighborhoods, ugly black
security bars across every entrance in the house were the norm.
There were many instances when people were burned alive in their
houses because they were not able to get out when a fire started.
The firemen were not able to get the bars off in time.

Between the drug epidemic, white flight, black flight, and the recession, Detroit stood on the threshold of disaster. Entire business districts went from being bustling commercial strips to bombed-out-looking eyesores. Entire neighborhoods disappeared. Downtown looked like a ghost town in the evenings and on the weekends as stores and businesses closed their doors. I must accept responsibility for the part I played in helping to bring our once great city to such a low point. The drugs I used and sold along with the other crimes I committed contributed to the blighted conditions of the city. I would work just as hard and long after becoming free from addiction attempting to help restore the city.

It appeared that at least the heroin epidemic was slowly coming to an end. Young people, having seen the effects of the drugs on their older brothers and sisters, their mothers and fathers, and their community, grew to despise the white powder. They would have no part of the devilish chemical.

We had no way of knowing at the time, but an even more insidious and deadly enemy waited at the gate. The effects of this enemy would make King Heroin look like a sissy. Many of those who had played such a prominent part in the proliferation of heroin throughout the community would be the first to fall. Many of the dope-dealing millionaires I knew were buzzing about a new way to get high off of cocaine. Freebasing cocaine had become all the rage among players. You may recall that the famed comedian Richard Pryor set himself on fire while engaging in this act. Before now, no one thought that cocaine was addictive, so those who would never think of using heroin freely used cocaine. It was looked upon back then as the chic, recreational drug of the rich and famous. Freebasing involved taking the white powder cocaine through a simple chemical process using easily acquired chemicals that turned it into a smokable rock form. Cocaine was different from heroin in that once a heroin user got his fill of the drug his appetite for the drug was usually satisfied. He could then go about his business until it was time to get high again, usually about a half a day. If a person attempted to use too much, the result was a drug overdose.

Cocaine, however, created an insatiable hunger for itself. It was virtually impossible to overdose from it. Also, the high only lasted for a short time. Researchers conducted an experiment using small monkeys to study the contrasting effects of heroin and cocaine. The habitat was set up so that one monkey could freely administer heroin to himself whenever he wanted. Another monkey was set up in a similar habitat and given the same access to cocaine. The heroin-addicted monkey was observed to go over to the machine that contained the drug, administering himself a dose of heroin. After he had received a satisfying dose, he went about his business grooming himself and even having sex with his partner.

The cocaine-addicted monkey, though, was observed standing at the machine that contained the drug repeatedly ingesting the drug. In fact, the cocaine-addicted monkey refused to leave the machine. He constantly tapped the button that administered the drug until his heart burst.

Freebasers were known to go through thousands of dollars in one sitting. Some men and women, like Sweet Bee, who I believe had amassed a million dollars or more, became paupers seemingly overnight. They thought the good times would roll forever. They didn't. Freebasing was a very involved and expensive process. The average person could not afford to indulge in this tremendously euphoric high. It would be another three years before bosses of the drug world would come up with a cheap smokable form of cocaine, which would be called *crack*.

Desperate for money, I went by Henry's looking for work. The upholstery business had gotten so bad that Henry only had enough work for himself and Deborah. They were barely keeping the doors open. Henry informed me that he did not have any work for me. He paid me $25 he had owed me from some previous work I had done. On his front counter was a copy of the local newspaper. Sometimes there were ads for furniture upholsterers in the want ad section of the paper. There was an ad for an experienced upholsterer in the nearby suburb of Dearborn. I called the number and was given an appointment for an interview.

The next day I caught the bus to the shop, which was located on Schafer Highway and Tireman. The name of the shop was Gramp's Furniture Clinic. One man, by the name of Don, operated a furniture refinishing operation in the rear of the building with his crew, while the man to whom I had applied for a job operated a small upholstery operation in the front of the building with one employee. The man I was to see was named Mark Torrie. He was a tall, gangly white man about my own age. He wore his hair in a long, dark mop about the length the Beatles had worn theirs years earlier.

Mark questioned me about my upholstery skills and experience. Satisfied that I qualified for the job, he hired me. He would pay me piecework, by the week, without a check in the hole. This meant that I would receive a check at the end of the week based on the work I produced. Cool!

Then Mark got weird on me. He told me that he was a Christian, and that God had instructed him to place the ad in the newspaper for an upholsterer. Currently, he did not have quite enough work to support another upholsterer but was confident that since God had given him this instruction his work would increase. Now, I had never heard anyone speak in terms of God having spoken directly to him. *This guy is a kook,* I thought to myself. It didn't matter though. He could have been the Boston Strangler for all I cared. I needed the work. This was a chance for me to make it through the winter at least.

I started work the next day. Upon arriving at the shop, I met Mike's only other employee, a short, curly-haired Italian-American by the name of Tommie Gerraldi, also about my own age. I was twenty-eight at the time. He was a lot friendlier than our boss was. No more than forty minutes into the workday after Mark had gotten me set up at my work station, he started telling me about how he had been a drug addict. Mark had been a hippie-type doper for quite a number of years. His drug use involved mostly marijuana, speed, and psychedelic drugs such as LSD. I viewed those drugs as relatively lightweight compared to my own experience. One day he met Jesus and God miraculously healed him of his addiction. Now he really had my attention.

I had never heard anyone talk about God in these terms. Hearing that God had an interest in miraculously healing a hippie doper was totally foreign to me. Before, I thought God only healed people in the movies—that it involved lepers and blind people, not white dopers. I had wanted to go to church for months. I believed that it would help me to change my life. I wanted desperately to change. I somehow knew that if ever I was to get my life on track it would mean returning to the God of my youth, the God of my mother. Quite frankly, though, I had forgotten the way back—I had traveled so far from home. I could no longer distinguish the voice of the Shepherd. Besides that, I didn't really believe that God had any real interest in someone like me, because I had never before seen a dopefiend saved by grace.

Every Saturday I told myself that I would get up in the morning and go to church. Every Sunday I woke up around 1:00 P.M. with an alcohol hangover and heroin withdrawal symptoms. At this point I was not deeply addicted to heroin in the physical sense. My addiction was more psychological.

The psychological addiction to heroin is the most powerful aspect of the drug, however. I have heard many stories of men and women who were addicted to heroin before going to prison. They stayed in prison for four or five years. The whole time they were in prison they did not use drugs. While they were on the bus on the way home from prison, they once again began to experience withdrawal symptoms. I had a similar experience when I returned home from prison after being locked up for a year. Actually, the vast majority of men and women who are addicted before going to prison will relapse soon after being released. While I did not use heroin everyday during this time, I used it every time I got my hands on a few dollars.

Mark told an amazing tale of how God had "delivered" him from his former lifestyle. God had given him an entirely new life, he told me. When Mark was finished with his story, Tommie began. Tommie told me he was an ex-offender who had been addicted to heroin. OK! Now my ears were sticking straight up. Talk to me, now. Tommie had been half of a salt and pepper (one black—one white) con man team in Detroit's Cass Corridor, one of Detroit's worst areas. He and his black partner preyed upon the elderly in that area. They were eventually caught and sent to jail. His partner, a repeat offender, received prison time while Tommie was sent to the Detroit House of Correction, which we called DeHoCo, to serve almost a year sentence.

While in jail, a friend of his mother began to visit Tommie. This man was a Christian who attended Fairlane Assembly of God Church, a Pentecostal denomination. This man assured Tommie that God had the power to heal him of his addiction and change his life forever. *Therefore, if any man be in Christ, he is a new creature: old things are passed away; behold, all things are become new.* (2 Corinthians 5:17) Through this man's ministry, Tommie accepted Christ as his personal Savior. He never looked back from that time on. He got out of jail and began to attend that church. He later got married, had a child, and seemed to have a very satisfying family life.

These men spoke in strange terms to me. I had had a lot of people in my life tell me that I needed to go to church. The church was supposed to be able to help me. The preacher was supposed to be able to help me. As a matter of fact, I had attended church on a number of occasions since coming home from prison. Shortly after coming home, I had even rejoined the church I attended as a child. However, I did not find the power to stop using drugs or running the streets. No one there understood my plight. There was no support system there for me. I left the church after about a month. Going to church had not helped me. Failing in this attempt only served to make me feel more hopeless.

No one talked to me, though, in terms of having a personal encounter with Christ. Yes, I had trusted Him to save my soul when I was nine years old. It should be obvious that I believe in the doctrine of eternal security, once saved always saved. But I had no idea I could have this kind of personal encounter with Him regarding the issues I faced in my life. My relationship with Him consisted of calling upon Him when I was in trouble. He always helped me, but I never reciprocated.

These two men witnessed to me endlessly. For the first time in my life, Christian conversation, Christian music, and Christian radio programming for nine hours a day surrounded me. The Sunday after I started at Gramps, I went to church for the first time in years. I hung in the background that first Sunday.

I never admitted to being an active drug user to Mark and Tommie. I told them that I was a member of a church, which was true. In most Baptist churches, once you were a member you stayed on the rolls until you died or joined another church. I had done neither. They were not fooled, though. They just kept coming at me, talking to me about this strange concept called deliverance. I had tried on so many occasions to free myself from the snare that held me captive. I tried cold turkey, methadone, other medications, substance-abuse counseling. I never got better, only worse. Now these guys were telling me that all I needed was to turn my life, my will over to Christ and He would heal me.

The thing that impressed me the most about these two young, godly men was not their words, but their lives. I marveled seeing how God had been able to turn their lives around. And what God had done for Tommie and Mark, I began to believe He could do for me.

So one day of the second week I worked for Mike, as I walked to the bus stop on my way home, I began talking to God as I had never done before. "God," I began, "I see what You have done for Tommie and Mark. God, I didn't know that You could do anything like that," I continued. "God, I didn't know You cared about us drugs addicts in that way. Lord, I know that I have turned away from You. I know that You helped me on so many occasions throughout my life. I made You promises and broke them all," I confessed. "But Lord, if You will take these drugs out of my life, if You will *deliver* me from this life I've been living, I promise that this time I will really serve You. I promise that I will tell others about You wherever I go." I began to sob as I continued down the street, pouring my heart out to God.

As I walked down that street in the cool drizzling rain that fall evening, crying out to God to save my miserable life, suddenly it was as if a great burden was lifted from my shoulders. I seemed to become strangely light. I was filled with a sense of joy and peace I had never known in my entire life. I began to laugh and cry all at the same time. It was almost like in the movies when a miracle occurred: heaven opens up and angels sing hallelujah. I didn't hear any angels singing, but I learned later that they did sing at that moment. *Likewise, I say unto you, there is joy in the presence of the angels of God over one sinner that repenteth.* (Luke 15:10) I knew that God had heard and answered my prayer. I knew that I would never use drugs or participate in a criminal lifestyle again. *He also brought me up out of a horrible pit, out of the miry clay, and set my feet upon a rock, and established my goings. He has put a new song in my mouth— Praise to our God; Many will see it and fear, and will trust in the Lord.* (Psalm 40: 2, 3) Praise God, I have been healed!

When I arrived home that night, I told Mike, my brother, what had happened and that I intended to begin to serve the Lord. Mike stared at me with a puzzled look on his face. Then with the most serious of tones he began, "You are starting to lose your mind. I have seen this a lot of times in prison," he assured me. "Whenever a guy is about to lose his mind, he starts getting religious."

"Well, Mike," I rebutted, "if I am crazy now, what have I been for the last thirteen years? I'll tell you what," I continued. "If this is what you call crazy, I'll take it hands down over what I had any day." Mike just sat on the daybed shaking his head. He was sure that I was headed for the mental ward at Detroit Receiving.

I called Mamma that same night. "Mamma, I'm coming back to the church," I informed her. I used the expression "back to church" because saying words and phrases like "the Lord" and "Jesus" did not yet fit right on my tongue. For so long I had used it for only profane expressions and lies. It would take a while for me to adjust. Mamma was silent for a while. "Hello? Hello? Mamma, did you hear what I said?" I shouted into the mouthpiece of the phone. "Lawd ha' mercy," was all the response she was able to muster. She was in shock. "Thank You, Jesus," she continued. "Mamma," I continued, "God has healed me of drug addiction. It was so wonderful, Mamma. I was walking down the street talking to Him, and He healed me just like that. I know I am healed," I exclaimed.

I could hear Dad in the background asking her what had happened. He no doubt thought I was in trouble again. "Our baby son is coming back to the church," she told Dad. "He say that God done healed him of dope addiction, and he coming back to the church." I could only hear silence in the background. I wondered if Dad had suffered a heart attack and died hearing the news.

This encounter with God caused me to totally lose interest in drugs. I had absolutely no desire to get high for the first time in thirteen years. The world seemed brighter than it ever had before. I had no idea what the future held for me, but I wasn't worried about it either. Again I showed up at the church I had attended as a child, the church Mamma and other relatives still attended. The Good Shepherd had patiently, persistently, so lovingly protected me for all those years. In all that time, I never received any serious injuries. I never was shot or stabbed. I never shot or stabbed anyone else. This is almost unheard of for the kind of life I lived. *Yea, though I walk through the valley of the shadow of death, I shall fear no evil for thou art with me.* Surely God had been with me all that time, even though I did not know it at the time.

This time I did not hang in the background. I carefully scoped the church, recognizing so many faces that I had not seen in years. Some of them were young people I had attended Sunday school with and served on the usher board with as a youngster. Most of them were women. Most of the young men had left at some point as I had done. Others were older adults who had offered me guidance as a child. It was so good to see them all looking so well. I wondered what their lives had been like for the past thirteen years I had been out of the church living among the wolves.

The service was upbeat and inspiring. Then at the end of the service as the choir sang, Rev. Page "opened the doors of the church." This is an expression used in traditional black churches. It means that the church is at that time ready to take in new members. In other churches this part of the service is called an invitation to discipleship, altar call, or salvation appeal. It is unfortunate that this vague term is used, because many times people who have no background in the church want to give their hearts to Christ, want to join the church, but do not understand what is happening during this part of the service.

I understood, though. I leapt from my seat on the red-cushioned pew and bounded down the aisle amidst a chorus of "praise the Lords" by the church members, seeing a young man walk forward apparently to join the church. I could not afford to get my chemically straightened hair done that week, so I wore it in a ponytail. At that time I had a full beard. I put together the best-looking outfit I could find in my depleted wardrobe. I must have looked a little rough around the edges standing there. Also standing at the altar were several others who had come forward. Rev. Page questioned all of us individually regarding the reason we came forward. When my time came, I jubilantly proclaimed, "I strayed away from the church for a long time. I have been in the streets for thirteen years. Now I am coming home." This brought on a chorus of "Thank You, Jesus," "Hallelujahs," and "Praise the Lords" from the congregation. Rev. Page, the undershepherd, heartily shook my hand, welcoming me back to the sheepfold.

Mamma had told me how many people in the church had been praying for me all those years I had been in the streets. She had not kept secret the fact that her children were in trouble out in the world. Instead, she thought it a wiser course to solicit the prayers of the saints. I thank God that Mamma had the courage to do that. Many parents and family members try to keep secret the fact that their loved one is involved in the streets, drugs, or is in prison. Thus they forfeit the power of the prayers of the righteous. Mamma had deacons, trustees, preachers who didn't even know me, my cousins who were in the church, my old Sunday school teachers, everybody she could enlist joining her in prayer for my brothers and sister and me.

Knowing that people didn't recognize me, I decided to play a game with them. I walked up to my cousin Betty who had been singing in the choir. "Lady, you don't know who I am, do you?" I teased. I didn't realize at the time how hard I must have looked. I hope I didn't frighten her. Betty just stood there, all 5' of her looking at me in bewilderment. "Who is this knucklehead?" she must have wondered to herself. Realizing that she would never guess who I was, I finally revealed my identity to her. "It's me, Joe," I proclaimed. Her mouth dropped wide open. Looking deep into my eyes, she exclaimed, "Lord have mercy, it is you, Joe." She grabbed me and gave me a big hug, her head only reaching about to my lower chest.

I rushed around the church looking for everyone I recognized and profusely thanked them for praying for me. I blurted out the shortest, crudest version of my healing experience, then rushed to the next person. Meanwhile, Betty had rounded up the rest of her family to greet me. When I made my way back to where she was, I recognized her now adult children, my cousins, and her husband, John. Jeanetta, who was the oldest, lived in Virginia with her husband and three children, and was not there. I was greeted by Chuckie, the next oldest, Violet and her husband and two daughters, and Carlton, the youngest. John stood there with a look of wonder on his face. Also, I found Betty's brother who also was named John. John had directed the choir that day. He still had on his choir robe. He gave me his biggest bear hug to let me know how happy he was to see me. I was back in church, back in the fold, and so happy to be there.

I learned so much from Betty and Mamma about assisting a drug-addicted ex-offender through transition to a wholesome lifestyle. Shortly after I came back to church, Betty invited me to her house for "game night." Before this I did not think that a person could have fun without using drugs or being involved in some kind of illicit activity. I came to the Lord believing I would never again in life have any fun. I envisioned myself sitting in church stone-faced, singing slow, mournful Christian songs. As my friend and colleague Bob Vann put it, I had "awfullized" sobriety.

At game night, Betty had invited a number of family members and other Christian friends. We sat around her dining room table playing all kinds of board games. Betty and others prepared an assortment of tasty snacks that we enjoyed all during that evening. I had a natural ball playing the games, eating, and talking with the others. It was possible to have big fun without sinning. These times of fellowship helped me perhaps more than anything else I experienced during my early days of transition.

Mamma showed me by her interactions with men and women in the neighborhood who had gone through hard times how to love unconditionally. She was a mentor to many women on her street. She even mentored a woman from our church who was recently released from prison. Mamma allowed this woman to move in with her until she found her a flat down the street. She held this woman, Margarette, accountable to her transition goals. These principles I learned from Mamma and Betty I would later integrate into ex-offender programs I later had the privilege of starting.

I was in church every time the door opened. I attended eight o'clock service, Sunday school, eleven o'clock service, and whatever program the church had going on Sunday evening. I attended mid-week service and Saturday morning prayer. On the first Sunday of each month, the church observed the Lord's Supper and baptism during a separate service at four o'clock in the afternoon. Between services, the older women in the church, the mothers, prepared a potluck meal so they did not have to go home between the services. I even hung out with the mothers and learned how to make some of their favorite dishes.

I called Dianna, telling her of my healing, deliverance, and rededication of my life to Christ. "That's nice," she responded. She had no idea I had any background in the church. I must have been one of the worst-acting people she had known at that point. Dianna and Tony came back to Detroit for a short visit. She stated that she was not ready to return to live in Detroit just yet. "Look, Dianna, I know I have been a terrible father to Tony and mate to you. All that is different now. I have given my life to God. We can be a family now. I want to get married and raise our son right," I told her. Strangely, she seemed less enthusiastic about my proposal than when we had discussed marriage before. She and Tony returned to Saginaw.

In about a couple of weeks, Dianna called to inform me that she did not plan to return to Detroit, nor would she marry me. She had found another guy in Saginaw and liked the prospects of her future with him better. She could not get into the religion that I talked so freely and enthusiastically about. Dianna was not a hard drug user, although she drank and smoked marijuana. She loved to party, though. She had constantly expressed her desire for me to stop using heroin. Now, however, I had gone too far. In her mind, I had gone from one extreme to another. While she did not want to be tied to a drug addict for life, she did not want to be hooked up with a religious fanatic either.

Dianna did not have the strong background in the church I had. She was only twenty years old at the time. She wanted to have some fun in her life. Going to church all the time and talking about Jesus was not her idea of fun. She had been very gracious to me by allowing me to live in her apartment. She had helped me and encouraged me a great deal. If it were not for her kindness, I don't know if I would have made it long enough to show up at Gramps that day. I certainly bore no grudges toward her. She made her decision. We remained friends, agreeing to work together to raise our son.

My twenty-ninth birthday fell on Tuesday, December 1, 1981. As I walked into the upholstery shop, Mark was quite sullen. He informed me that work was slow and he would have to lay me off. He appeared quite perplexed as he sat there explaining to me what led him to his decision. "I know that God told me to place that ad in the paper," he began. "I thought that meant that my work was going to increase, but it didn't. I don't have enough work for both Tommie and you. So since you were the last one hired, I have to let you go."

Mark was very narrow in his thinking. He had little regard for black Baptist churches—black Christian churches in general, for that matter. To him if it wasn't white Pentecostal it wasn't right. I had tried to relate my dramatic experience to him on several occasions. However, because I attended a black Baptist church and had not gone through the same steps he had gone through in his own conversion experience, he discounted the validity of my healing and deliverance. Tommie was different. He knew that something significant had occurred in my life. "Joe's going to be a preacher," he once suggested to Mark. Mark simply looked at him blankly and grunted. It is still hard for me to understand how a person can be so godly in some aspects of their lives, yet so prejudiced and narrow in others.

I wanted to jump up and down and shout to Mark, "Yes, God told you to put that ad in the paper so that I could come here to hear the message of deliverance and be healed," but I felt it would be a matter of casting pearls before swine. I left the shop never to see Mark again. I saw Tommie on a few occasions after I left the shop. I lost track of him shortly after that, however. Mark's statement that God had instructed him to place the ad in the paper was a great confirmation to me that God would not abandon me. I firmly believed that since God had gone to such great measures to preserve my life and to bring me out of the darkness, He had a work for me to do. He would take care of me.

It was as if I had finally heard the voice of the Good Shepherd. He had been calling to me all those years. I had ignored Him or failed to hear His voice. But now I was hearing it loud and clear. The words of this great song express what I experienced perfectly:

> I heard the voice of Jesus say, "Come unto me and rest.
> Lay down, My weary one, lay down thy head upon My breast."
> I came to Jesus as I was—
> I was weary, worn, and sad;
> I found in Him a resting place,
> And He has made me glad.

I didn't have a job. Dianna had brought Tony to Detroit to live with me for several months. I was a single parent. Winter was not around the corner but just up the street. But I wasn't worried, because I was back in the sheepfold. The Devil couldn't get to me as long as I remained here. *Surely goodness and mercy shall follow me all the days of my life: and I will dwell in the house of the Lord forever. Amen.*

Epilogue

God really was merciful to me. He provided for Tony and me in some wonderful ways. As always, He used His people to do it. With only a tack hammer and a pair of cutting shears, I began my own upholstering business. Upon learning I was an upholsterer, many people in the church began to give me work to do. Greater New Mt. Moriah was a large church, having a membership of about 2,500 members at that time. For a while the people at Mt. Moriah made up my entire clientele. I believe that many of them were not all that interested in getting work done, but merely wanted to help me out in a manner that was dignifying to me. I operated that business for nearly ten years as I put myself through college on a part-time basis in preparation for ministry.

I began to minister in the Wayne County Jail about six months after returning to the Lord. In August of 1982, Dad died of a massive stroke. A good friend of mine, Kay Warren, led Dad to Christ on his deathbed. I went to visit him the following day, asking him if he understood what he had done. He nodded his head yes. Dad died a few days after that. I will rejoice when I see him in heaven. Mamma went home to be with her Lord in the spring of 1996.

Shortly after Dad died, I felt that God was calling me into the ministry. Although Tony and I were living comfortably in a rented house on the northwest side, I moved back in with Mamma so that she would not be alone in that bad neighborhood. As I sat in Dad's favorite chair reading the book of Isaiah, I came to the 61st chapter, verse 4: *The Spirit of the LORD GOD is upon me because the LORD hath anointed me to preach good tidings unto the meek; he hath sent me to bind up the brokenhearted, to proclaim liberty to the captives, and the opening of the prison to them that are bound.* Those words leapt off the page at me. I sensed that God was telling me through this verse what my purpose in life was. I was licensed to preach that fall.

Eventually, God brought a wonderful young woman into my life I had known as a teenager at church. Sharon Ray was a lovely, shy young woman about my age. We were both too shy as teenagers to have ever spoken much to each other. On July 27, 1995, she became my wife. Including Tony, we have four children: Stephen, AnnDrea, and Gabrielle.

I graduated from William Tyndale College in 1988 with a Bachelor of Religious Education Degree, majoring in Urban Studies and Bible. I graduated cum laude (actually, "thank you, Lordy"), and was elected to Who's Who in American Colleges and Universities, and Delta Epsilon Chi, National Honor Society. In 1994, I graduated from Wayne State University with a Master of Arts degree in Applied Sociology.

God has given me the opportunity to join Him in service by working as a substance abuse counselor and caseworker at the Detroit Rescue Mission and Christian Guidance Center, working with drug-addicted ex-offenders. After graduating from Tyndale College, I had the opportunity to work there for a year as an admissions counselor. After that, I worked at Teen Ranch Family Service, a Christian child welfare agency that ministers to abused and neglected children, as a fund developer. All the while I remained active in prison ministry as a volunteer.

In 1992, Prison Fellowship Ministries (PF) hired me as the Area Director for Southeastern Michigan. After being in that position for about four months, PF moved me into the position of Director of Detroit Transition of Prisoners (TOP). TOP at the time was in its conceptual stage. It was established to create a model that would be used to assist Christian ex-prisoners in their transition from prison to the free world. TOP has since become a very successful model program for the nation.

In July 1997, I became the Managing Director for Network for Life (NFL) and Detroit TOP. NFL is a national ex-offender program of PF. Through a network of church volunteers, chaplains, local businesspeople, community agencies, and others, NFL helps men and women whose lives have been devastated by drugs, crime, and prison to make a successful transition back into the community, becoming contributing members of society.

I have worked with substance abusers specifically for several years and continue to work with drug-addicted prisoners and ex-prisoners. In my seventeen years of working with this population, I have come to the conclusion that the only way for a person to successfully overcome this truly terrible affliction is to have a significant encounter with God. God, I am convinced, is the only One who can bring wholeness to a life once it has taken this tragic turn. Now, I am not saying that everyone has to have the same experience I had. I have met some that have. Most have not. What I am saying is that whatever process a person goes through, be it a twelve-step program, the cognitive behavioral approach, or some other program, one can and must at some point experience the total healing of God in this area of their lives.

On this point I realize that I differ greatly with Alcoholics Anonymous and other programs that teach that addiction is a disease from which one can never be cured. Recovery is a process that never ends, they teach. They say that a person must make it one day at a time. This philosophy flies in the face of Scripture. God's Word tells us that if any man is in Christ, he is a new creation. Old things have passed away, and all is become new. It also tells us that to be free in Christ is to be free indeed. So how can we say to substance abusers they can never be free from this crippling affliction? I fear that more people have been hurt by this philosophy than helped over the years.

Personally, I have watched in sadness as many individuals struggle to be free from alcohol and drug abuse "one day at a time." They live in constant trepidation that today will be that day that it will all come apart. Addicted people fail repeatedly, having been convinced that they can never receive healing and must carry this awful burden for the rest of their lives. Recovery is a lifelong process, they are taught. I have not met many people who can make it one day at a time, forever, Now I understand that Scripture teaches that we should live one day at a time. That is true. When I refer to "one day at a time" here I am speaking strictly within the context of chemical dependency.

I no longer recommend that people attend secular-based twelve-step groups. While the principles of the twelve steps are solid, biblically based principles, the program has taken "God" out of its vocabulary, leaving it impotent when it comes to helping people overcome their addictions. In many twelve step groups, people are not even allowed to bring Bibles to the meetings. They are stopped at the door and told that they must leave God's Word outside. This is truly sad since this movement started out with a biblical base. No wonder they have no power.

Substance abuse professionals teach that substance abuse is an illness like any other illness. Well, if that is true, as the late Dr. J. Vernon McGee used to say, it is the only illness you can purchase at your corner liquor store. I add that it is the only one you can purchase on the corner in rock or powder form. True, it is a sickness, one that is sometimes referred to as sin-sickness. It is a spiritual problem that can only be successfully addressed by spiritual means.

There are some very good Christ-centered twelve-step programs, such as Alcoholics for Christ (AC), that I freely recommend to those seeking help. These groups have been very successful as they work with local churches using the Word of God to restore the lives that have been ripped to shreds by the enemy of our souls, the Devil. These groups are also effective in helping to educate the loved ones of a substance abuser so they can be more wise in their dealings with them. So, let no one tell you there is no hope for you or your loved one. Don't be so easy to give up on them.

I am thankful that my mother and others never gave up on me, but kept me in constant prayer for thirteen long years. I praise the Good Shepherd for not giving up on me even when I had given up on Him. He watched over me in a truly marvelous way. Now He allows me to work with Him in the business of restoring broken lives. He has taken me through some thrilling experiences since I have been allowing Him to lead me. Hallelujah!

Perhaps the greatest thrill of my life, though, is the ability to be a good husband and father. Last summer, my wife, Sharon, and Tony's mother, Dianna (who is now a Christian), and I joyfully attended the high school graduation of our son. Had not God so graciously healed and delivered me, his chances of making it in life would have been quite slim. Tony is now awaiting acceptance into the Detroit Poclice Department training academy. Should he make it, he will be the first Williams to ride in the front seat of a police cruiser.

Surely goodness and mercy shall follow me all the days of my life. And I will dwell in the house of the Lord forever. Amen.

Be Sure to Read All the Other Books in the NEW Lift Every Voice Imprint

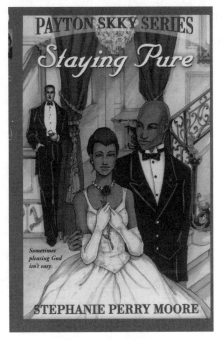

Staying Pure

Staying Pure addresses the pressures African-American girls face to stay physically pure and remain devoted to God. Not only is Payton Skky popular, but she is also dating the best looking guy at her high school. While he is pressuring her to sleep with him, Payton is content to wait, convinced that he is the one she will marry. As the pressure increases Payton starts to wonder if waiting is really worth it, especially since she believes that they will always be together. If she had sleeps with him will they be together forever? Payton struggles with these questions and with exactly what is God's plan for and meaning of purity.

Quality Paperback 0-8024-4236-6

Sober Faith

Payton Skky has gotten over her ex-boyfriend and
is now dating a strong Christian, Tad, who   is
keeping her accountable. Her friends, however, are
still struggling with their identity and exactly what
is right and wrong. Chasing after fun they discover
alcohol and drugs. They spend time experimenting
without thinking of the consequences. Payton
wants to help her friends realize the dangers in
what they are doing, but she also wants to be
accepted by them. Can she do both? How far is too
far? What about Tad, who doesn't approve of what
Payton's friends are doing? Can she help her
friends without compromising her faith?

Quality Paperback 0-8024-4237-4

Plant Seeds of Hope in the Youth of Your Community

Planting Seeds of Hope
How to Reach a New Generation of African-Americans With the Gospel

African American youth are looking for role models they can trust. *Planting Seeds of Hope* is written to help youth workers, pastors, parents, and others who care about reaching young people with the hope of the Gospel. Among other topics, this book explores how to earn the trust of young people, place youth in a position to know the God who created them, and work with the community. Our young people are worth the effort it takes to present them to God and to prepare them for a future bright with promise and hope.

Quality Paperback 0-8024-5428-3